Ancient Texts and the Bible
Book 5 - Easy Reader Edition

In The Beginning...
From Egypt to Goshen

Minister 2 Others

Ancient Texts and the Bible
Book 5

In The Beginning...
From Egypt to Goshen

Easy Reader Edition

In The Beginning... From Egypt to Goshen
ISBN 978-1-947751-23-1

Ancient texts compiled for this series:

The Bible
King James Version 1769

The Book of Enoch
An English translation by Dr. Laurence,
Archbishop of Cashel,
Formerly professor of Hebrew at Oxford, 1833

The Book of Jasher
Faithfully translated 1840
From the original Hebrew into English
Published by J.H. Parry & Company 1887

The Book of Jubilees
By R.H. Charles, Oxford: Clarendon Press, 1913

Ancient Texts and the Bible

series include:

Book 1: In The Beginning... From Adam to Noah

Book 2: In The Beginning... From Noah to Abraham

Book 3: In The Beginning... From Abraham to Israel

Book 4: In The Beginning... From Israel to Egypt

Book 5: In The Beginning... From Egypt to Goshen

Book 6: Israel... From Goshen to Sinai

Book 7: Israel... From Sinai to the Tabernacle

Book 8: Israel... Through the Book of Leviticus

Book 9: Israel... Through the Book of Numbers

Book 10: Israel... Through the Book of Joshua

Table of Contents:

Forward

The **Ancient Texts and the Bible** series synchronizes the manuscripts of Enoch, Jasher, and Jubilees into the Bible, making one complete storyline. The books are interwoven using the Torah as the backbone, and the extra-biblical texts as the fleshing out of that backbone.

The fifth book in the series contains Genesis chapters 40-50, the book of Jasher chapters 47-65, and the book of Jubilees chapters 39-46.

Though the language in the writings have been updated, replacing words like "*thou*" and "*thine*" with words like "*you*" and "*your*", the integrity of the verses remain.

The "*Easy Reader*" edition is for those who just want to read the storyline and enjoy the journey. The stop signs and complex formatting have been removed so one may merely focus upon the story being told.

The *Expanded Edition* of **Ancient Texts and the Bible** was created for the more studious reader. The various manuscripts have the following formatting applied to them in this edition:

the Bible - Regular

THE BOOK OF ENOCH - ALL CAPITALS

the Book of Jasher - Italics

<u>the Book of Jubilees - Underlined</u>

Where one of the extra-biblical texts reiterates the Bible, the phrase is then put in a **bold font**. Where two manuscripts overlap each other exclusive of the Bible, then both fonts are used. For instance, where Jasher and Jubilees intercept, the text is then formatted as *Italics and Underlined.*

The stop sign is another element to the *Expanded Edition* that is not seen in the *Easy Reader*. This image points to contradictions in the content. Printed versions also contain page numbers within the stop sign revealing the page where contradictory information is located, and vice versa. This information was not feasible to place in the e-book versions since the page numbers vary depending on the font size the reader chooses. Following, is an example from each edition:

Easy Reader Edition:

(Genesis 41:7) (...Jasher 48:5) (...Jubilees 40:1...)
And the seven thin ears devoured the seven rank and full ears. And Pharaoh awoke out of his sleep, and, behold, it was a dream.

Expanded Edition:

(Genesis 41:7) (...Jasher 48:5) (...Jubilees 40:1...)
And the seven ***thin ears devoured the*** seven rank and ***full ears.*** **And Pharaoh awoke** out of his sleep, and, behold, it was a ***dream***.

Whichever you choose, may you ***Enjoy the Journey***!

Prologue

(Jasher 47:1)
And Isaac the son of Abraham was still living in those days in the land of Canaan; he was very aged, one hundred and eighty years old, and Esau his son, the brother of Jacob, was in the land of Edom, and he and his sons had possessions in it among the children of Seir.

(Jasher 47:2)
And Esau heard that his father's time was drawing near to die, and he and his sons and household came to the land of Canaan, to his father's house, and Jacob and his sons went forth from the place where they dwelt in Hebron, and they all came to their father Isaac, and they found Esau and his sons in the tent.

(Jasher 47:3)
And Jacob and his sons sat before his father Isaac, and Jacob was still mourning for his son Joseph.

(Jasher 47:4)
And Isaac said to Jacob, Bring your sons here to me and I will bless them; and Jacob brought his eleven children before his father Isaac.

(Jasher 47:5)
And Isaac placed his hands upon all the sons of Jacob, and he took hold of them and embraced them, and kissed them one by one, and Isaac blessed them on that day, and he said to them, May the God of your fathers bless you and increase your seed like the stars of heaven for number.

(Jasher 47:6)
And Isaac also blessed the sons of Esau, saying, May God cause you to be a dread and a terror to all that will behold you, and to all your enemies.

(Jasher 47:7)
And Isaac called Jacob and his sons, and they all came and sat before Isaac, and Isaac said to Jacob, The Lord God of the whole earth said to me, To your seed will I give this land for an inheritance if your children keep my statutes and my ways, and I will perform to them the oath which I swore to your father Abraham.

(Jasher 47:8)
Now therefore my son, teach your children and your children's children to fear the Lord, and to go in the good way which will please the Lord your God, for if you keep the ways of the Lord and his statutes the Lord will also keep to you his covenant with Abraham, and will do well with you and your seed all the days.

(Jasher 47:9)
And when Isaac had finished commanding Jacob and his children, he gave up the ghost and died, and was gathered to his people.

(Jasher 47:10)
And Jacob and Esau fell upon the face of their father Isaac, and they wept, and Isaac was one hundred and eighty years old when he died in the land of Canaan, in Hebron, and his sons carried him to the cave of Machpelah, which Abraham had bought from the children of Heth for a possession of a burial place.

(Jasher 47:11)
And all the kings of the land of Canaan went with Jacob and Esau to bury Isaac, and all the kings of Canaan showed Isaac great honor at his death.

(Jasher 47:12)
And the sons of Jacob and the sons of Esau went barefooted round about, walking and lamenting until they reached Kireath-arba.

(Jasher 47:13)
And Jacob and Esau buried their father Isaac in the cave of Machpelah, which is in Kireath-arba in Hebron, and they buried him with very great honor, as at the funeral of kings.

(Jasher 47:14)
And Jacob and his sons, and Esau and his sons, and all the kings of Canaan made a great and heavy mourning, and they buried him and mourned for him many days.

(Jasher 47:15)
And at the death of Isaac, he left his cattle and his possessions and all belonging to him to his sons; and Esau said to Jacob, Behold I pray you, all that our father has left we will divide it in two parts, and I will have the choice, and Jacob said, We will do so.

(Jasher 47:16)
And Jacob took all that Isaac had left in the land of Canaan, the cattle and the property, and he placed them in two parts before Esau and his sons, and he said to Esau, Behold all this is before you, choose you to yourself the half which you will take.

(Jasher 47:17)
And Jacob said to Esau, Hear, I pray, what I will speak to you, saying, The Lord God of heaven and earth spoke to our fathers Abraham and Isaac, saying, To your seed will I give this land for an inheritance forever.

(Jasher 47:18)
Now therefore, all that our father has left is before you, and behold all the land is before you; choose from them what you desire.

(Jasher 47:19)
If you desire the whole land take it for you and your children forever, and I will take the riches, and if you desire the riches, take it to you, and I will take this land for me and for my children to inherit it forever.

(Jasher 47:20)
And Nebayoth, the son of Ishmael, was then in the land with his children, and Esau went on that day and consulted with him, saying.

(Jasher 47:21)
Thus has Jacob spoken to me, and thus has he answered me, now give your advice and we will hear.

(Jasher 47:22)
And Nebayoth said, What is this that Jacob hath spoken to you? Behold all the children of Canaan are dwelling securely in their land, and Jacob said he will inherit it with his seed all the days.

(Jasher 47:23)
Go now therefore and take all your father's riches and leave

Jacob your brother in the land, as he has spoken.

(Jasher 47:24)
And Esau rose up and returned to Jacob, and did all that Nebayoth the son of Ishmael had advised; and Esau took all the riches that Isaac had left, the souls, the beasts, the cattle and the property, and all the riches; he gave nothing to his brother Jacob; and Jacob took all the land of Canaan, from the brook of Egypt to the river Euphrates, and he took it for an everlasting possession, and for his children and for his seed after him forever.

(Jasher 47:25)
Jacob also took from his brother Esau the cave of Machpelah, which is in Hebron, which Abraham had bought from Ephron for a possession of a burial place for him and his seed forever.

(Jasher 47:26)
And Jacob wrote all these things in the book of purchase, and he signed it, and he testified all this with four faithful witnesses.

(Jasher 47:27)
And these are the words which Jacob wrote in the book, saying: The land of Canaan and all the cities of the Hittites, the Hivites, the Jebusites, the Amorites, the Perizzites, and the Gergashites, all the seven nations from the river of Egypt to the river Euphrates.

(Jasher 47:28)
And the city of Hebron Kireath-arba, and the cave which is in it, the whole Jacob bought from his brother Esau for value, for a possession and for an inheritance for his seed after him forever.

(Jasher 47:29)
And Jacob took the book of purchase and the signature, the command and the statutes and the revealed book, and he placed them in an earthen vessel in order that they should remain for a long time, and he delivered them into the hands of his children.

(Jasher 47:30)
Esau took all that his father had left him after his death from his brother Jacob, and he took all the property, from man and beast, camel and donkey, ox and lamb, silver and gold, stones and bdellium, and all the riches which had belonged to Isaac the son of Abraham; there was nothing left which Esau did not take to himself, from all that Isaac had left after his death.

(Jasher 47:31)
And Esau took all this, and he and his children went home to the land of Seir the Horite, away from his brother Jacob and his children.

(Jasher 47:32)
And Esau had possessions among the children of Seir, and Esau returned not to the land of Canaan from that day forward.

(Jasher 47:33)
And the whole land of Canaan became an inheritance to the children of Israel for an everlasting inheritance, and Esau with all his children inherited the mountain of Seir.

Genesis: Chapter Forty

(Jasher 46:1) (Jubilees 39:14...)
In those days Joseph was still confined in the prison house in the land of Egypt. And he remained there two years.

(Genesis 40:1...) (Jasher 46:2)
And it came to pass at that time after these things, that the attendants of Pharaoh were standing before him, the chief of the butlers and the chief of the bakers which belonged to the king of Egypt.

(Jasher 46:3)
And the butler took wine and placed it before the king to drink, and the baker placed bread before the king to eat, and the king drank of the wine and ate of the bread, he and his servants and ministers that ate at the king's table.

(...Genesis 40:1) (Jasher 46:4)
And the butler of the king of Egypt and his baker offended their lord the king of Egypt. While they were eating and drinking, the butler and the baker remained there, and Pharaoh's ministers found many flies in the wine, which the butler had brought, and stones of nitre were found in the baker's bread.

(Genesis 40:2) (...Jubilees 39:14...)
And Pharaoh king of Egypt was wroth against two of his officers, against the chief of the butlers, and against the chief of the bakers.

(Genesis 40:3) (...Jubilees 39:14)
And he put them in ward in the house of the captain of the guard, the chief cook, into the prison, the place where Joseph was bound.

(Genesis 40:4) (Jasher 46:5) (Jubilees 39:15)
And the captain of the guard charged Joseph with them, and he served them: and they continued a season in ward, Pharaoh's officers were in confinement one year.

(Genesis 40:5) (Jasher 46:6...) (Jubilees 39:16...)
And at the end of the year, they dreamed a dream both of them, each man his dream in one night, in the place of confinement where they were, each man according to the interpretation of his dream, the chief butler and the chief baker of the king of Egypt, which were bound in the prison.

(Genesis 40:6) (...Jasher 46:6)
And Joseph came in to them in the morning as usual, and looked on them, and, behold, they were dejected and sad.

(Genesis 40:7) (Jasher 46:7...)
And he asked Pharaoh's officers that were with him in the ward of his lord's house, saying, Why do you look so sad and dejected today?

(Genesis 40:8) (...Jasher 46:7)
And they said to him, We have dreamed a dream, and there is no interpreter of it. And Joseph said to them, Do not interpretations belong to God? Tell me them, I pray, and God shall give you an answer of peace as you desire.

(Genesis 40:9) (Jasher 46:8...) (...Jubilees 39:16...)
And the chief butler told his dream to Joseph, and said to

him, I saw in my dream, behold, a large vine was before me;

(Genesis 40:10) (...Jasher 46:8)

And in the vine, there were three branches: and it was as though it speedily budded, and her blossoms shot forth and reached a great height; and the clusters thereof brought forth ripe grapes:

(Genesis 40:11) (Jasher 46:9...)

And Pharaoh's cup was in my hand: and I took the grapes, and pressed them into Pharaoh's cup, and I gave the cup into Pharaoh's hand and he drank.

(Genesis 40:12) (...Jasher 46:9...)

And Joseph said to him, This is the interpretation of it: The three branches that were upon the vine are three days:

(Genesis 40:13) (Jasher 46:10...)

Yet within three days shall Pharaoh lift up your head, the king will order you to be brought out and restore you to your place: and you shall deliver Pharaoh's cup into his hand, after the former manner when you were his butler.

(Genesis 40:14) (...Jasher 46:10...)

But think on me when it shall be well with you, and show kindness, I pray, to me, and make mention of me to Pharaoh, and bring me out of this house:

(Genesis 40:15) (...Jasher 46:10, 11)

For indeed I was stolen away out of the land of Canaan from the Hebrews and was sold for a slave in this place: and here also that which was told you concerning my master's wife is false, for I have done nothing that they should put me into the dungeon. And the butler answered Joseph, saying, If the king deal well with me as at first, as you last interpreted to me, I will do all that you desire, and get you brought out of this dungeon.

(Genesis 40:16) (Jasher 46:12, 13...) (...Jubilees 39:16)
And when the chief baker saw that the interpretation was good, that Joseph had accurately interpreted the butler's dream, he also approached, and related the whole of his dream to Joseph. And he said to Joseph, I also was in my dream, and I saw, behold, I had three white baskets on my head:

(Genesis 40:17) (...Jasher 46:13)
And I looked, and behold in the uppermost basket there was of all manner of baked foods for Pharaoh; and behold the birds ate them out of the basket on my head.

(Genesis 40:18) (Jasher 46:14...)
And Joseph answered and said to him, This is the interpretation thereof: The three baskets which you saw are three days:

(Genesis 40:19) (...Jasher 46:14)
Yet within three days shall Pharaoh lift up your head from off you, and shall hang you on a tree; and the birds shall eat your flesh from off you, as you saw in your dream.

(Jasher 46:15)
In those days, the queen was about to be delivered, and upon that day she bore a son to the king of Egypt, and they proclaimed that the king had gotten his first-born son and all the people of Egypt together with the officers and servants of Pharaoh rejoiced greatly.

(Genesis 40:20...) (Jasher 46:16)
And it came to pass upon the third day of his birth, which was

Pharaoh's birthday, that he made a feast to all his officers and his servants, for the hosts of the land of Zoar and of the land of Egypt:

(Jasher 46:17)
And all the people of Egypt and the servants of Pharaoh came to eat and drink with the king at the feast of his son, and to rejoice at the king's rejoicing.

(...Genesis 40:20)
And Pharaoh lifted up the head of the chief butler and of the chief baker among his servants.

(Genesis 40:21) (Jubilees 39:17...)
And he restored the chief butler to his butlership again; and he gave the cup into Pharaoh's hand:

(Genesis 40:22) (...Jubilees 39:17)
But he hanged the chief baker: Thus as Joseph interpreted to them so it befell them, as Joseph had interpreted to them.

(Jasher 46:18)
And all the officers of the king and his servants were rejoicing at that time for eight days at the feast, and they made merry with all sorts of musical instruments, with timbrels and with dances in the king's house for eight days.

(Genesis 40:23) (Jasher 46:19) (Jubilees 39:18)
Yet the chief butler, to whom Joseph had interpreted his dream, did not remember Joseph, but he forgot him in the prison, and he did not mention him to the king as he had promised, although he had informed him what would befall him, how Joseph had told him, for he forgot for this thing

was from the Lord in order to punish Joseph because he had trusted in man.

(Jasher 46:20)
And Joseph remained after this in the prison house two years, until he had completed twelve years.

Genesis: Chapter Forty-One

(Genesis 41:1) (Jasher 48:2) (Jubilees 40:1...)

And it came to pass at the end of two full years from Joseph interpreting the dreams of the king's servants, that at that time Pharaoh king of Egypt was sitting upon his throne in the land of Egypt. And in those days, Pharaoh lay in his bed and Pharaoh dreamed two dreams in one night concerning a famine which was to be in all the land: and Pharaoh saw in his dream that, behold, he stood by the river of Egypt.

(Genesis 41:2) (Jasher 48:3)

And while he was standing he saw and behold, there came up out of the river seven well favored, and fat cows; and they fed in a meadow.

(Genesis 41:3) (Jasher 48:4...)

And, behold, seven other cows came up after them out of the river, ill-favored and skinny; and stood by the other cows on the brink of the river.

(Genesis 41:4) (...Jasher 48:4, 5...)

And the seven ill-favored and skinny cows ate up the seven well favored and fat cows and still their appearance was ill as at first. So Pharaoh awoke.

(Genesis 41:5) (...Jasher 48:5...)

And he slept and dreamed the second time: and he saw and behold, seven ears of corn came up on one stalk, rank and good.

(Genesis 41:6) (...Jasher 48:5...)

And, behold, seven, thin ears and blasted with the east wind sprung up after them.

(Genesis 41:7) (...Jasher 48:5) (...Jubilees 40:1...)

And the seven thin ears devoured the seven rank and full ears. And Pharaoh awoke out of his sleep, and, behold, it was a dream.

(Genesis 41:8...) (Jasher 48:6) (...Jubilees 40:1...)

And it came to pass in the morning that the king remembered his dreams, and his spirit was sadly troubled on account of his dreams; and the king hastened and sent and called for all the interpreters of dreams that were in Egypt, and magicians of Egypt, and all the wise men thereof: and they came and stood before Pharaoh.

(Jasher 48:7)

And the king said to them, I have dreamed dreams, and there is none to interpret them; and they said to the king, relate your dreams to your servants and let us hear them.

(...Genesis 41:8...) (Jasher 48:8) (...Jubilees 40:1...)

And Pharaoh told them his two dreams; and they all answered and said with one voice to the king, may the king live forever; and this is the interpretation of your dreams.

(Jasher 48:9)

The seven good kine which you saw denote seven daughters that will be born to you in the latter days, and the seven kine which you saw come up after them, and swallowed them up, are for a sign that the daughters which will be born to you will all die in the life-time of the king.

(Jasher 48:10)
And that which you saw in the second dream of seven full good ears of corn coming up upon one stalk, this is their interpretation, that you will build to yourself in the latter days seven cities throughout the land of Egypt; and that which you saw of the seven blasted ears of corn springing up after them and swallowing them up while you beheld them with thine eyes, is for a sign that the cities which you will build will all be destroyed in the latter days, in the life-time of the king.

(Jasher 48:11)
And when they spoke these words the king did not incline his ear to their words, neither did he fix his heart upon them, for the king knew in his wisdom that they did not give a proper interpretation of the dreams; and when they had finished speaking before the king, the king answered them, saying, What is this thing that you have spoken to me? Surely you have uttered falsehood and spoken lies; therefore now give the proper interpretation of my dreams, that you may not die.

(Jasher 48:12)
And the king commanded after this, and he sent and called again for other wise men, and they came and stood before the king, and the king related his dreams to them, and they all answered him according to the first interpretation, and the king's anger was kindled and he was very wroth, and the king said to them, Surely you speak lies and utter falsehood in what you have said.

(Jasher 48:13)
And the king commanded that a proclamation should be issued throughout the land of Egypt, saying, It is resolved by the king and his great men, that any wise man who knows and understands the interpretation of dreams, and will not come this day before the king, shall die.

(Jasher 48:14)
And the man that will declare to the king the proper interpretation of his dreams, there shall be given to him all that he will require from the king. And all the wise men of the land of Egypt came before the king, together with all the magicians and sorcerers that were in Egypt and in Goshen, in Rameses, in Tachpanches, in Zoar, and in all the places on the borders of Egypt, and they all stood before the king.

(Jasher 48:15)
And all the nobles and the princes, and the attendants belonging to the king, came together from all the cities of Egypt, and they all sat before the king, and the king related his dreams before the wise men, and the princes, and all that sat before the king were astonished at the vision.

(Jasher 48:16)
And all the wise men who were before the king were greatly divided in their interpretation of his dreams; some of them interpreted them to the king, saying, The seven good kine are seven kings, who from the king's issue will be raised over Egypt.

(Jasher 48:17)
And the seven bad kine are seven princes, who will stand up against them in the latter days and destroy them; and the seven ears of corn are the seven great princes belonging to Egypt, who will fall in the hands of the seven less powerful princes of their enemies, in the wars of our lord the king.

(Jasher 48:18)
And some of them interpreted to the king in this manner, saying, The seven good kine are the strong cities of Egypt, and the seven bad kine are the seven nations of the land of

Canaan, who will come against the seven cities of Egypt in the latter days and destroy them.

(Jasher 48:19)
And that which you saw in the second dream, of seven good and bad ears of corn, is a sign that the government of Egypt will again return to your seed as at first.

(Jasher 48:20)
And in his reign the people of the cities of Egypt will turn against the seven cities of Canaan who are stronger than they are, and will destroy them, and the government of Egypt will return to your seed.

(Jasher 48:21)
And some of them said to the king, This is the interpretation of your dreams; the seven good kine are seven queens, whom you will take for wives in the latter days, and the seven bad kine denote that those women will all die in the lifetime of the king.

(Jasher 48:22)
And the seven good and bad ears of corn which you saw in the second dream are fourteen children, and it will be in the latter days that they will stand up and fight among themselves, and seven of them will smite the seven that are more powerful.

(Jasher 48:23)
And some of them said these words to the king, saying, The seven good kine denote that seven children will be born to you, and they will slay seven of your children's children in the latter days; and the seven good ears of corn which you saw in the second dream, are those princes against whom seven other less powerful princes will fight and destroy them

in the latter days, and avenge your children's cause, and the government will again return to your seed.

(...Genesis 41:8) (...Jubilees 40:1)
But there was none that could interpret them to Pharaoh.

(Jasher 48:24)
And the king heard all the words of the wise men of Egypt and their interpretation of his dreams, and none of them pleased the king.

(Jasher 48:25)
And the king knew in his wisdom that they did not altogether speak correctly in all these words, for this was from the Lord to frustrate the words of the wise men of Egypt, in order that Joseph might go forth from the house of confinement, and in order that he should become great in Egypt.

(Jasher 48:26)
And the king saw that none among all the wise men and magicians of Egypt spoke correctly to him, and the king's wrath was kindled, and his anger burned within him.

(Jasher 48:27)
And the king commanded that all the wise men and magicians should go out from before him, and they all went out from before the king with shame and disgrace.

(Jasher 48:28)
And the king commanded that a proclamation be sent throughout Egypt to slay all the magicians that were in Egypt, and not one of them should be suffered to live.

(Jasher 48:29)
And the captains of the guards belonging to the king rose up, and each man drew his sword, and they began to smite the magicians of Egypt, and the wise men.

(Jasher 48:30)
And after this, Merod, chief butler to the king, came and bowed down before the king and sat before him.

(Genesis 41:9) (Jasher 48:31) (Jubilees 40:2...)
Then the chief butler remembered Joseph and spoke of him to Pharaoh, saying, May the king live forever, and his government be exalted in the land. I remember my faults this day:

(Genesis 41:10) (Jasher 48:32)
Pharaoh was wroth with his servants in those days, now two years past, and put me in ward in the captain of the guard's house, and I was for some time in the ward, both me and the chief baker:

(Genesis 41:11) (Jasher 48:34)
And in some time after when we were in the ward, we dreamed a dream in one night, I and he; we dreamed each man according to the interpretation of his dream.

(Genesis 41:12) (Jasher 48:33, 35)
And there was there with us a young man, an Hebrew, servant to the captain of the guard, his name was Joseph, for his master had been angry with him and placed him in the house of confinement, and he attended us there. And we came in the morning and we told them to that servant, and he interpreted to us our dreams; to each man according to his dream he interpreted.

(Genesis 41:13) (Jasher 48:36)

And it came to pass, as he interpreted to us, so it was; me he restored to my office, and him he hanged; there fell not to the ground any of his words.

(Jasher 48:37)

And now therefore my lord and king do not slay the people of Egypt for naught; behold that slave is still confined in the house by the captain of the guard his master, in the house of confinement.

(Jasher 48:38)

If it pleases the king let him send for him that he may come before you and he will make known to you, the correct interpretation of the dream which you dreamed.

(Jasher 48:39)

And the king heard the words of the chief butler, and the king ordered that the wise men of Egypt should not be slain.

(Genesis 41:14) (Jasher 48:40, 41) (...Jubilees 40:2...)

Then Pharaoh sent his servants and called Joseph, and the king said to them, Go to him and do not terrify him lest he be confused and will not know to speak properly. And the servants of the king went to Joseph, and they brought him hastily out of the dungeon: and he was shaven and changed his raiment, and came in to Pharaoh.

(Jasher 48:42)

And the king was sitting upon his royal throne in a princely dress girt around with a golden ephod, and the fine gold which was upon it sparkled, and the carbuncle and the ruby and the emerald, together with all the precious stones that were upon the king's head, dazzled the eye, and Joseph wondered greatly at the king.

(Jasher 48:43)
And the throne upon which the king sat was covered with gold and silver, and with onyx stones, and it had seventy steps.

(Jasher 48:44)
And it was their custom throughout the land of Egypt, that every man who came to speak to the king, if he was a prince or one that was estimable in the sight of the king, he ascended to the king's throne as far as the thirty-first step, and the king would descend to the thirty-sixth step, and speak with him.

(Jasher 48:45)
If he was one of the common people, he ascended to the third step, and the king would descend to the fourth and speak to him, and their custom was, moreover, that any man who understood to speak in all the seventy languages, he ascended the seventy steps, and went up and spoke till he reached the king.

(Jasher 48:46)
And any man who could not complete the seventy, he ascended as many steps as the languages which he knew to speak in.

(Jasher 48:47)
And it was customary in those days in Egypt that no one should reign over them, but who understood to speak in the seventy languages.

(Jasher 48:48)
And when Joseph came before the king he bowed down to the ground before the king, and he ascended to the third step, and the king sat upon the fourth step and spoke with Joseph.

(Genesis 41:15) (Jasher 48:49, 50)

And Pharaoh said to Joseph, I have dreamed a dream, and there is none that can interpret it properly, and I commanded this day that all the magicians of Egypt and the wise men thereof, should come before me, and I related my dreams to them, and no one has properly interpreted them to me. And after this, this day I have heard say of you, that you are a wise man, and you can understand a dream to correctly interpret every dream that you hear.

(Genesis 41:16) (Jasher 48:51...)

And Joseph answered Pharaoh, saying, Let Pharaoh relate his dreams that he dreamed; surely the interpretations belong to God; It is not in me: God shall give Pharaoh an answer of peace.

(Genesis 41:17) (...Jasher 48:51...) (...Jubilees 40:2)

And Pharaoh related his two dreams to Joseph, the dream of the kine, and the dream of the ears of corn. And Pharaoh said to Joseph, In my dream, behold, I stood on the bank of the river:

(Genesis 41:18)

And, behold, there came up out of the river seven cows, fat and well favored; and they fed in a meadow:

(Genesis 41:19)

And, behold, seven other cows came up after them, poor and very ill favored and skinny, such as I never saw in all the land of Egypt for badness:

(Genesis 41:20)

And the lean and the ill favored cows ate up the first seven fat cows:

(Genesis 41:21)

And when they had eaten them up, it could not be known that they had eaten them; but they were still ill favored, as at the beginning. So I awoke.

(Genesis 41:22)

And I saw in my dream, and, behold, seven ears came up in one stalk, full and good:

(Genesis 41:23)

And, behold, seven ears, withered, thin, and blasted with the east wind, sprung up after them:

(Genesis 41:24) (...Jasher 48:51)

And the thin ears devoured the seven good ears: and I told this to the magicians; but there was none that could declare it to me. And the king left off speaking.

(Jasher 48:52)

And Joseph was then clothed with the spirit of God before the king, and he knew all the things that would befall the king from that day forward, and he knew the proper interpretation of the king's dream, and he spoke before the king.

(Jasher 48:53...)

And Joseph found favor in the sight of the king, and the king inclined his ears and his heart, and he heard all the words of Joseph.

(Genesis 41:25) (...Jasher 48:53) (Jubilees 40:3...)

And Joseph said to Pharaoh, Do not imagine that they are two dreams, for the dream of Pharaoh is only one dream: God has showed Pharaoh in his dream, what he is about to do throughout the land. And this is the proper interpretation of your dream:

(Genesis 41:26) (Jasher 48:54...)
The seven good cows are seven years; and the seven good ears are seven years: the dream is one.

(Genesis 41:27) (...Jasher 48:54)
And the seven thin and ill favored cows that came up after them are also seven years; and the seven empty ears blasted with the east wind shall be seven years of famine.

(Genesis 41:28)
This is the thing which I have spoken to Pharaoh: What God is about to do he is showing to Pharaoh.

(Genesis 41:29) (Jasher 48:55...) (...Jubilees 40:3...)
Behold, there come seven years of great plenty throughout all the land of Egypt:

(Genesis 41:30) (...Jasher 48:55...) (...Jubilees 40:3...)
And there shall arise after them seven years of famine; and all the plenty shall be forgotten in the land of Egypt; and the famine shall consume the inhabitants of the land;

(Genesis 41:31) (...Jasher 48:55) (...Jubilees 40:3)
And the plenty shall not be known in the land by reason of that famine following; for it shall be very grievous, such a famine as has not been in all the land.

(Genesis 41:32) (Jasher 48:56)
And for that, the king dreamed one dream, the dream was doubled to Pharaoh twice; it is because the thing is established by God, and God will shortly bring it to pass.

(Genesis 41:33) (Jasher 48:57)

Now therefore, I will give you counsel and deliver your soul and the souls of the inhabitants of the land from the evil of the famine, let Pharaoh look out throughout your kingdom for a man very discreet and wise, who knows all the affairs of government, and set him to superintend over the land of Egypt.

(Genesis 41:34) (Jasher 48:58...) (Jubilees 40:4...)

Let Pharaoh do this, and let the man whom you place over Egypt appoint officers under him over all the land of Egypt, and take up the fifth pare of the land of Egypt in the seven plenteous years.

(Genesis 41:35) (...Jasher 48:58) (...Jubilees 40:4...)

And let them gather and let them store up all the food in every city throughout the days of those good years that come, and lay up corn under the hand of Pharaoh, and deposit it in your appointed stores and let them keep food in the cities.

(Genesis 41:36) (Jasher 48:59) (...Jubilees 40:4)

And that food shall be for store to the land against the seven years of famine, which shall be in the land of Egypt; that it may be found for you and your people and your whole land, and that you and the land does not perish through the famine, for it will be very severe.

(Jasher 48:60)

Let all the inhabitants of the land be also ordered that they gather in, every man the produce of his field, of all sorts of food, during the seven good years, and that they place it in their stores, that it may be found for them in the days of the famine and that they may live upon it.

(Jasher 48:61)
This is the proper interpretation of your dream, and this is the counsel given to save your soul and the souls of all your subjects.

(Jasher 48:62)
And the king answered and said to Joseph, Who says and who knows that your words are correct? And he said to the king, This shall be a sign for you respecting all my words, that they are true and that my advice is good for you.

(Jasher 48:63)
Behold your wife sits this day upon the stool of delivery, and she will bear you a son and you will rejoice with him; when your child shall have gone forth from his mother's womb, your first born son that has been born these two years back shall die, and you will be comforted in the child that will be born to you this day.

(Jasher 48:64)
And Joseph finished speaking these words to the king, and he bowed down to the king and he went out, and when Joseph had gone out from the king's presence, those signs which Joseph had spoken to the king came to pass on that day.

(Jasher 48:65)
And the queen bore a son on that day and the king heard the glad tidings about his son, and he rejoiced, and when the reporter had gone forth from the king's presence, the king's servants found the first born son of the king fallen dead upon the ground.

(Jasher 48:66)
And there was great lamentation and noise in the king's

house, and the king heard it, and he said, What is the noise and lamentation that I have heard in the house? And they told the king that his first born son had died; then the king knew that all Joseph's words that he had spoken were correct, and the king was consoled for his son by the child that was born to him on that day as Joseph had spoken.

~ ~ ~

(Jasher 49:1)
After these things, the king sent and assembled all his officers and servants, and all the princes and nobles belonging to the king, and they all came before the king.

(Jasher 49:2)
And the king said to them, Behold you have seen and heard all the words of this Hebrew man, and all the signs which he declared would come to pass, and not any of his words have fallen to the ground.

(Jasher 49:3)
You know that he has given a proper interpretation of the dream, and it will surely come to pass, now therefore take counsel, and know what you will do and how the land will be delivered from the famine.

(Jasher 49:4)
Seek now and see whether the like can be found, in whose heart there is wisdom and knowledge, and I will appoint him over the land.

(Jasher 49:5)
For you have heard what the Hebrew man has advised concerning this to save the land therewith from the famine, and I know that the land will not be delivered from the famine but with the advice of the Hebrew man, him that advised me.

(Jasher 49:6)
And they all answered the king and said, The counsel which the Hebrew has given concerning this is good; now therefore, our lord and king, behold the whole land is in your hand, do that which seems good in your sight.

(Jasher 49:7)
Him whom you choose, and whom you in your wisdom know to be wise and capable of delivering the land with his wisdom, him shall the king appoint to be under him over the land.

(Jasher 49:8)
And the king said to all the officers: I have thought that since God has made known to the Hebrew man all that he has spoken, there is none so discreet and wise in the whole land as he is; if it seems good in your sight I will place him over the land, for he will save the land with his wisdom.

(Jasher 49:9)
And all the officers answered the king and said, But surely it is written in the laws of Egypt, and it should not be violated, that no man shall reign over Egypt, nor be the second to the king, but one who has knowledge in all the languages of the sons of men.

(Jasher 49:10)
Now therefore our lord and king, behold this Hebrew man can only speak the Hebrew language, and how then can he be

over us the second under government, a man who does not even know our language?

(Jasher 49:11)
Now we pray you send for him, and let him come before you, and prove him in all things, and do as you see fit.

(Jasher 49:12)
And the king said, It shall be done tomorrow, and the thing that you have spoken is good; and all the officers came on that day before the king.

(Jasher 49:13)
And on that night the Lord sent one of his ministering angels, and he came into the land of Egypt to Joseph, and the angel of the Lord stood over Joseph, and behold Joseph was lying in the bed at night in his master's house in the dungeon, for his master had put him back into the dungeon on account of his wife.

(Jasher 49:14)
And the angel roused him from his sleep, and Joseph rose up and stood upon his legs, and behold the angel of the Lord was standing opposite to him; and the angel of the Lord spoke with Joseph, and he taught him all the languages of man in that night, and he called his name Jehoseph.

(Jasher 49:15)
And the angel of the Lord went from him, and Joseph returned and lay upon his bed, and Joseph was astonished at the vision which he saw.

(Jasher 49:16)
And it came to pass in the morning that the king sent for all

his officers and servants, and they all came and sat before the king, and the king ordered Joseph to be brought, and the king's servants went and brought Joseph before Pharaoh.

(Jasher 49:17)
And the king came forth and ascended the steps of the throne, and Joseph spoke to the king in all languages, and Joseph went up to him and spoke to the king until he arrived before the king in the seventieth step, and he sat before the king.

(Jasher 49:18)
And the king greatly rejoiced on account of Joseph, and all the king's officers rejoiced greatly with the king when they heard all the words of Joseph.

(Genesis 41:37) (Jasher 49:19...) (Jubilees 40:5...)
And the Lord gave Joseph favor and mercy and the thing was good in the eyes of Pharaoh, and in the eyes of all his servants to appoint Joseph to be second to the king over the whole land of Egypt.

(Genesis 41:38) (...Jubilees 40:5)
And Pharaoh said to his servants, Can we find such a one as this is, a man in whom the Spirit of God is?

(Genesis 41:39) (...Jasher 49:19, 20)
And Pharaoh said to Joseph, Now you gave me counsel to appoint a wise man over the land of Egypt, in order with his wisdom to save the land from the famine; now forasmuch as God has showed you all this, and all the words which you have spoken, there is none so discreet and wise as you are:

(Genesis 41:40...) (Jasher 49:21...) (Jubilees 40:7...)
And Pharaoh magnified him and said to him: You shall be over

my house, you shall be second to me, and according to your word shall be all the affairs of my government, and according to your word shall all my people be ruled:

(...Genesis 41:40) (Jasher 49:22) (...Jubilees 40:7...)
Also from under your hand shall my servants and officers receive their salary which is given to them monthly, and to you shall all the people of the land bow down; only in the throne will I be greater than you.

(Jubilees 40:6...)
And he appointed him the second in all his kingdom.

(Genesis 41:41) (...Jubilees 40:6...)
And Pharaoh said to Joseph, See, I have set you over all the land of Egypt.

(Genesis 41:42) (Jasher 49:23) (...Jubilees 40:7)
And Pharaoh took off his ring from his hand, and put it on Joseph's hand, and the king arrayed him in vestures of fine linen, in a princely garment, with byssus garments, and he put a golden crown upon his head, and put a gold chain about his neck; and proclaimed before him El El wa Abirer.

(Genesis 41:43...) (Jasher 49:24) (...Jubilees 40:6)
And the king commanded his servants, and they made him to ride in the second chariot belonging to the king, that went opposite to the king's chariot, and he caused him to ride upon a great and strong horse from the king's horses, and to be conducted through the streets of the land of Egypt.

(Jasher 49:25)
And the king commanded that all those that played upon timbrels, harps and other musical instruments should go

forth with Joseph; one thousand timbrels, one thousand mecholoth, and one thousand nebalim went after him.

(Jasher 49:26)
And five thousand men, with drawn swords glittering in their hands, and they went marching and playing before Joseph, and twenty thousand of the great men of the king girt with girdles of skin covered with gold, marched at the right hand of Joseph, and twenty thousand at his left, and all the women and damsels went upon the roofs or stood in the streets playing and rejoicing at Joseph, and gazed at the appearance of Joseph and at his beauty.

(Jasher 49:27)
And the king's people went before him and behind him, perfuming the road with frankincense and with cassia, and with all sorts of fine perfume, and scattered myrrh and aloes along the road, and twenty men proclaimed these words before him throughout the land in a loud voice:

(Jasher 49:28)
Do you see this man whom the king has chosen to be his second? The affairs of government shall be regulated by him, and he that transgresses his orders, or that does not bow down before him to the ground, shall die, for he rebels against the king and his second.

(...Genesis 41:43)
And they cried before him, Bow the knee: and Pharaoh made him ruler over all the land of Egypt.

(Jasher 49:29)
And when the heralds had ceased proclaiming, all the people of

Egypt bowed down to the ground before Joseph and said, May the king live, also may his second live; and all the inhabitants of Egypt bowed down along the road, and when the heralds approached them, they bowed down, and they rejoiced with all sorts of timbrels, mechol and nebal before Joseph.

(Jasher 49:30)
And upon his horse, Joseph lifted up his eyes to heaven, and called out and said, He raises the poor man from the dust, He lifts up the needy from the dunghill. O Lord of Hosts, happy is the man who trusts in you.

(Genesis 41:44) (Jasher 49:37...)
And Pharaoh said to Joseph, I am Pharaoh, and without you no man shall dare to lift up his hand or foot to regulate my people in all the land of Egypt.

(Genesis 41:45...) (...Jasher 49:21, 36) (Jubilees 40:10)
And your name no more shall be called Joseph, but Zaphnath Paaneah shall be your name; And Pharaoh called Joseph's name Zaphnathpaaneah. And the king sent to Potiphera and he took his young daughter and he gave him Asenath the daughter of Potipherah, the son of Ahiram, the daughter of the priest of On, the chief cook for a wife.

(...Jasher 49:37)
And the damsel was very comely, a virgin, one whom man had not known, and Joseph took her for a wife

(...Genesis 41:45) (Jasher 49:31)
And Joseph went out over all the land of Egypt with Pharaoh's servants and officers, and they showed him the whole land of Egypt and all the king's treasures.

(Jasher 49:32)
And Joseph returned and came on that day before Pharaoh, and the king gave to Joseph a possession in the land of Egypt, a possession of fields and vineyards, and the king gave to Joseph three thousand talents of silver and one thousand talents of gold, and onyx stones and bdellium and many gifts.

(Jasher 49:33)
And on the next day the king commanded all the people of Egypt to bring to Joseph offerings and gifts, and that he that violated the command of the king should die; and they made a high place in the street of the city, and they spread out garments there, and whoever brought anything to Joseph put it into the high place.

(Jasher 49:34)
And all the people of Egypt cast something into the high place, one man a golden ear- ring, and the other rings and ear-rings, and different vessels of gold and silver work, and onyx stones and bdellium he cast upon the high place; everyone gave something of what he possessed.

(Jasher 49:35)
And Joseph took all these and placed them in his treasuries, and all the officers and nobles belonging to the king exalted Joseph, and they gave him many gifts, seeing that the king had chosen him to be his second.

(Genesis 41:46) (Jasher 49:38) (Jubilees 40:11)
And Joseph was thirty years old on the day when he stood before Pharaoh king of Egypt. And Joseph went out from the presence of Pharaoh, and he became the king's second in Egypt and went throughout all the land of Egypt.

(Jasher 49:39)
And the king gave Joseph a hundred servants to attend him in his house, and Joseph also sent and purchased many servants and they remained in the house of Joseph.

(Jasher 49:40)
Joseph then built for himself a very magnificent house like to the houses of kings, before the court of the king's palace, and he made in the house a large temple, very elegant in appearance and convenient for his residence; three years was Joseph in erecting his house.

(Jasher 49:41)
And Joseph made to himself a very elegant throne of abundance of gold and silver, and he covered it with onyx stones and bdellium, and he made upon it the likeness of the whole land of Egypt, and the likeness of the river of Egypt that waters the whole land of Egypt; and Joseph sat securely upon his throne in his house and the Lord increased Joseph's wisdom.

(Jasher 49:42) (Jubilees 40:8)
And Joseph ruled over all the land of Egypt, and all the inhabitants of Egypt and all Pharaoh's servants and all his princes, and all who did the king's business loved Joseph exceedingly, for he walked in uprightness, for he was without pride and arrogance, and he had no respect of persons, and did not accept gifts, but he judged in uprightness all the people of the land. For this thing was from the Lord to Joseph.

(Jasher 49:43)
And Joseph had an army that made war, going out in hosts and troops to the number of forty thousand six hundred men, capable of bearing arms to assist the king and Joseph against the enemy, besides the king's officers and his servants and

inhabitants of Egypt without number.

(Jasher 49:44)
And Joseph gave to his mighty men, and to all his host, shields and javelins, and caps and coats of mail and stones for slinging.

(Jubilees 40:9)
And the land of Egypt was at peace before Pharaoh because of Joseph, for the Lord was with him, and gave him favor and mercy for all his generations before all those who knew him and those who heard concerning him, and Pharaoh's kingdom was well ordered, and there was no Satan and no evil person therein.

~ ~ ~

(Jasher 50:1)
At that time, the children of Tarshish came against the sons of Ishmael, and made war with them, and the children of Tarshish spoiled the Ishmaelites for a long time.

(Jasher 50:2)
And the children of Ishmael were small in number in those days, and they could not prevail over the children of Tarshish, and they were sorely oppressed.

(Jasher 50:3)
And the old men of the Ishmaelites sent a record to the king of Egypt, saying, Send I pray you to your servant's officers and hosts to help us to fight against the children of Tarshish, for we have been consuming away for a long time.

(Jasher 50:4)
And Pharaoh sent Joseph with the mighty men and host which were with him, and also his mighty men from the king's house.

(Jasher 50:5)
And they went to the land of Havilah to the children of Ishmael, to assist them against the children of Tarshish, and the children of Ishmael fought with the children of Tarshish, and Joseph smote the Tarshishites and he subdued all their land, and the children of Ishmael dwell therein to this day.

(Jasher 50:6)
And when the land of Tarshish was subdued, all the Tarshishites ran away, and came on the border of their brothers the children of Javan, and Joseph with all his mighty men and host returned to Egypt, not one man of them missing.

~ ~ ~

(Jubilees 40:12...)
And in that year Isaac died.

(Genesis 41:47) (Jasher 50:7) (...Jubilees 40:12)
And it came to pass at the revolution of the year, in the second year of Joseph's reigning over Egypt, the Lord gave great plenty throughout the land for seven years, as Joseph had spoken in the interpretation of Pharaoh's two dreams, according as Joseph had said. In the seven plenteous years the land of Egypt brought forth by handfuls, abundantly producing, one measure producing eighteen hundred measures, for the Lord blessed all the produce of the earth in those days for seven

years, and they ate and were greatly satisfied.

(Genesis 41:48) (Jasher 50:8)

And Joseph at that time had officers under him, and they gathered up all the food of the seven good years, which were in the land of Egypt, and laid up the food in the cities and they placed it in the treasuries of Joseph: the food of the field, which was round about every city, he laid up in the same.

(Jasher 50:9)

And at any time when they gathered the food Joseph commanded that they should bring the corn in the ears, and also bring with it some of the soil of the field, that it should not spoil.

(Genesis 41:49) (Jasher 50:10) (Jubilees 40:13)

And Joseph did according to this year by year, and he gathered corn into every city until they were full of corn as the sand of the sea for abundance, very much, until he left numbering and measuring it; for his stores were immense and it was without number for abundance.

(Jasher 50:11)

And also all the inhabitants of Egypt gathered all sorts of food in their stores in great abundance during the seven good years, but they did not do to it as Joseph did.

(Jasher 50:12)

And all the food which Joseph and the Egyptians had gathered during the seven years of plenty, was secured for the land in stores for the seven years of famine, for the support of the whole land.

(Jasher 50:13)
And the inhabitants of Egypt filled each man his store and his concealed place with corn, to be for support during the famine.

(Jasher 50:14)
And Joseph placed all the food that he had gathered in all the cities of Egypt, and he closed all the stores and placed sentinels over them.

(Genesis 41:50) (Jasher 50:15...)
And to Joseph were born two sons before the years of famine came, which Asenath the daughter of Potipherah priest of On bore to him.

(Genesis 41:51) (...Jasher 50:15...)
And Joseph called the name of the firstborn Manasseh: For God, he said, has made me forget all my toil, and all my father's house.

(Genesis 41:52) (...Jasher 50:15)
And the name of the second he called Ephraim: For God has caused me to be fruitful in the land of my affliction. And Joseph was thirty-four years old when he begot them.

(Jasher 50:16)
And the lads grew up and they went in his ways and in his instructions, they did not deviate from the way which their father taught them, either to the right or left.

(Jasher 50:17)
And the Lord was with the lads, and they grew up and had understanding and skill in all wisdom and in all the affairs of government, and all the king's officers and his great men

of the inhabitants of Egypt exalted the lads, and they were brought up among the king's children.

(Genesis 41:53) (Jasher 50:18...)
And the seven years of plenteousness, that was in the land of Egypt, were ended.

(Jasher 48:1)
In those days, after the death of Isaac, the Lord commanded and caused a famine upon the whole earth.

(Genesis 41:54) (...Jasher 50:18) (Jubilees 42:1, 2)
And the seven years of famine began to come into the land, after them, in the first year of the third week of the forty-fifth jubilee, according as Joseph had said: and the famine was in all lands; and the rain refused to be given to the earth, for none whatever fell. And the earth grew barren, but in all the land of Egypt there was bread for Joseph had gathered the seed of the land in the seven years of plenty and had preserved it.

(Jasher 50:19)
And all the people of Egypt saw that the famine had commenced in the land of Egypt, and all the people of Egypt opened their stores of corn for the famine prevailed over them.

(Jasher 50:20)
And they found all the food that was in their stores, full of vermin and not fit to eat, and the famine prevailed throughout the land, and all the inhabitants of Egypt came and cried before Pharaoh, for the famine was heavy upon them.

(Genesis 41:55...) (Jasher 50:21)
And when all the land of Egypt was famished, the people cried to Pharaoh for bread saying: Give food to your servants, and

wherefore shall we die through hunger before your eyes, even we and our little ones?

(Jasher 50:22)
And Pharaoh answered them, saying, And wherefore do you cry to me? Did not Joseph command that the corn should be laid up during the seven years of plenty for the years of famine? And wherefore did you not hearken to his voice?

(Jasher 50:23)
And the people of Egypt answered the king, saying, As your soul lives, our lord, your servants have done all that Joseph ordered, for your servants also gathered in all the produce of their fields during the seven years of plenty and laid it in the stores to this day.

(Jasher 50:24)
And when the famine prevailed over your servants we opened our stores, and behold all our produce was filled with vermin and was not fit for food.

(...Genesis 41:55) (Jasher 50:25)
And when the king heard all that had befallen the inhabitants of Egypt, the king was greatly afraid on account of the famine, and he was much terrified. And Pharaoh said to all the Egyptians, saying, Since all this has happened to you, go to Joseph; do whatever he says to you, do not transgress his commands.

(Genesis 41:56...)
And the famine was over all the face of the earth:

(Jasher 50:26) (Jubilees 42:3...)
And all the people of Egypt went forth and came to Joseph

that he might give them food, and said to him, Give to us food, and wherefore shall we die before you through hunger? For we gathered in our produce during the seven years as you commanded, and we put it in store, and thus has it befallen us.

(...Genesis 41:56) (Jasher 50:27) (...Jubilees 42:3)
And when Joseph heard all the words of the people of Egypt and what had befallen them, Joseph opened all the storehouses of the produce of the first year, and he sold it to the Egyptians for gold; and the famine waxed sore in the land of Egypt.

(Jasher 50:28)
And the famine prevailed throughout the land, and the famine was in all countries, but in the land of Egypt there was produce for sale.

(Jasher 50:29)
And all the inhabitants of Egypt came to Joseph to buy corn, for the famine prevailed over them, and all their corn was spoiled, and Joseph daily sold it to all the people of Egypt.

(Genesis 41:57) (Jasher 50:30)
And all the inhabitants of the land of Canaan and the Philistines, and those beyond the Jordan, and the children of the east and all the cities of the lands far and near heard that there was corn in Egypt, and all countries came into Egypt to Joseph to buy corn; because that the famine was so sore in all lands and famine prevailed over them.

(Jasher 50:31)
And Joseph opened the stores of corn and placed officers over them, and they daily stood and sold to all that came.

(Jasher 50:32)
And Joseph knew that his brothers also would come to Egypt to buy corn, for the famine prevailed throughout the earth. And Joseph commanded all his people that they should cause it to be proclaimed throughout the land of Egypt, saying,

(Jasher 50:33)
It is the pleasure of the king, of his second and of their great men, that any person who wishes to buy corn in Egypt shall not send his servants to Egypt to purchase, but his sons, and also any Egyptian or Canaanite, who shall come from any of the stores from buying corn in Egypt, and shall go and sell it throughout the land, he shall die, for no one shall buy but for the support of his household.

(Jasher 50:34)
And any man leading two or three beasts shall die, for a man shall only lead his own beast.

(Jasher 50:35)
And Joseph placed sentinels at the gates of Egypt, and commanded them, saying, Any person who may come to buy corn, suffer him not to enter until his name, and the name of his father, and the name of his father's father be written down, and whatever is written by day, send their names to me in the evening that I may know their names.

(Jasher 50:36)
And Joseph placed officers throughout the land of Egypt, and he commanded them to do all these things.

(Jasher 50:37)
And Joseph did all these things, and made these statutes, in order that he might know when his brothers should come to

Egypt to buy corn; and Joseph's people caused it daily to be proclaimed in Egypt according to these words and statutes which Joseph had commanded.

(Jasher 50:38)
And all the inhabitants of the east and west country, and of all the earth, heard of the statutes and regulations which Joseph had enacted in Egypt, and the inhabitants of the extreme parts of the earth came and they bought corn in Egypt day after day, and then went away.

(Jasher 50:39)
And all the officers of Egypt did as Joseph had commanded, and all that came to Egypt to buy corn, the gate keepers would write their names, and their fathers' names, and daily bring them in the evening before Joseph.

Genesis: Chapter Forty-Two

(Genesis 42:1) (Jasher 51:1) (Jubilees 42:4...)
Now the famine was very sore in the land of Canaan, and when Jacob saw that there was corn in Egypt, and he called to his sons to go to Egypt to buy corn, for upon them also the famine prevailed. Jacob said to his sons, Why do you look one on another?

(Genesis 42:2) (Jasher 51:2)
And he said to his sons, Behold, I have heard that there is corn in Egypt, and all the people of the earth go there to purchase, now therefore why will you show yourselves satisfied before the whole earth? Get down there, and buy for us from among those that come there; that we may live, and not die.

(...Jubilees 42:4...)
So Jacob sent his ten sons that they should procure food for him in Egypt;

(Genesis 42:3) (Jasher 51:3) (...Jubilees 42:4...)
And Joseph's ten brothers, the ten sons of Jacob, hearkened to the voice of their father, and they rose up to go down to buy corn from Egypt.

(Jasher 51:4)
And Jacob their father commanded them, saying, When you come into the city do not enter together in one gate, on account of the inhabitants of the land.

(Genesis 42:4) (Jasher 51:5) (...Jubilees 42:4...)
And the sons of Jacob went forth and they went to Egypt, and the sons of Jacob did all as their father had commanded them. But Jacob did not send Benjamin, Joseph's brother, with his brothers; for he said, Lest peradventure mischief befall him, an accident might befall him on the road like his brother. And ten of Jacob's sons went forth.

(Jasher 51:6)
And while the sons of Jacob were going on the road, they repented of what they had done to Joseph, and they spoke to each other, saying, We know that our brother Joseph went down to Egypt, and now we will seek him where we go, and if we find him we will take him from his master for a ransom, and if not, by force, and we will die for him.

(Genesis 42:5) (Jasher 51:3, 7) (...Jubilees 42:4)
And the sons of Jacob agreed to this thing and strengthened themselves on account of Joseph, to deliver him from the hand of his master. And the sons of Israel came to Egypt to buy corn among those that came: for the famine was in the land of Canaan. And when they came near to Egypt they separated from each other, and they came through ten gates of Egypt, and the gate keepers wrote their names on that day, and brought them to Joseph in the evening.

(Jasher 51:8...)
And Joseph read the names from the hand of the gate-keepers of the city, and he found that his brothers had entered at the ten gates of the city.

(Genesis 42:6...) (...Jasher 51:8)
And Joseph was the governor over the land, and he it was that sold to all the people of the land: and Joseph at that time commanded that it should be proclaimed throughout the land

of Egypt, saying,

(Jasher 51:9)
Go forth all ye store guards, close all the corn stores and let only one remain open, that those who come may purchase from it.

(Jasher 51:10)
And all the officers of Joseph did so at that time, and they closed all the stores and left only one open.

(Jasher 51:11)
And Joseph gave the written names of his brothers to him that was set over the open store, and he said to him, Whosoever shall come to you to buy corn, ask his name, and when men of these names shall come before you, seize them and send them, and they did so.

(Jasher 51:12)
And when the sons of Jacob came into the city, they joined together in the city to seek Joseph before they bought themselves corn.

(Jasher 51:13)
And they went to the walls of the harlots, and they sought Joseph in the walls of the harlots for three days, for they thought that Joseph would come in the walls of the harlots, for Joseph was very comely and well favored, and the sons of Jacob sought Joseph for three days, and they could not find him.

(Jasher 51:14)
And the man who was set over the open store sought for those names which Joseph had given him, and he did not find them.

(Jasher 51:15)
And he sent to Joseph, saying, These three days have passed, and those men whose names you gave to me have not come; and Joseph sent servants to seek the men in all Egypt, and to bring them before Joseph.

(Jasher 51:16)
And Joseph's servants went and came into Egypt and could not find them, and went to Goshen and they were not there, and then went to the city of Rameses and could not find them.

(Jasher 51:17)
And Joseph continued to send sixteen servants to seek his brothers, and they went and spread themselves in the four corners of the city, and four of the servants went into the house of the harlots, and they found the ten men there seeking their brother.

(...Genesis 42:6) (Jasher 51:18)
And those four men took them and brought them before him, and Joseph's brothers came, and bowed down themselves before him with their faces to the earth. And Joseph was sitting upon his throne in his temple, clothed with princely garments, and upon his head was a large crown of gold, and all the mighty men were sitting around him.

(Jasher 51:19)
And the sons of Jacob saw Joseph, and his figure and comeliness and dignity of countenance seemed wonderful in their eyes, and they again bowed down to him to the ground.

(Genesis 42:7) (Jasher 51:19..., 21)
And Joseph saw his brothers, and he knew them, but made himself strange to them, and spoke roughly to them; and he

said to them, Where do you come from? And they all answered and said, Your servants have come from the land of Canaan to buy food. For the famine prevails throughout the earth, and your servants heard that there was corn in Egypt, so they have come among the other comers to buy corn for their support.

(Genesis 42:8) (...Jasher 51:19) (Jubilees 42:5...)
And Joseph knew his brothers, but they did not know him for Joseph was very great in their eyes, therefore they knew him not.

(Genesis 42:9) (Jasher 51:22) (...Jubilees 42:5...)
And Joseph remembered the dreams which he dreamed of them, and he spoke to them and questioned them, and said to them, If you have come to purchase as you say, why do you come through ten gates of the city? It can only be that you are spies; you came to see the nakedness of the land. Have you not come to explore the approaches of the land?

(Genesis 42:10) (Jasher 51:23...)
And they all together answered Joseph, and said to him, Nay, my lord, but your servants came to buy food.

(Genesis 42:11) (...Jasher 51:23)
Your servants are twelve brothers, the sons of one man in the land of Canaan; and our father commanded us, saying, When you come to the city do not enter together at one gate on account of the inhabitants of the land; we are right, true men, your servants are not spies.

(Genesis 42:12) (Jasher 51:24)
And he again answered them and said to them, Nay, but that is the thing which I spoke to you, you have come to spy through the land, therefore you all came through ten gates of the city;

you came to see the nakedness of the land.

(Jasher 51:25)
Surely everyone that comes to buy corn goes his way, and you are already three days in the land, and what do you do in the walls of harlots in which you have been for these three days? Surely spies do like to these things.

(Genesis 42:13) (Jasher 51:26)
And they said to Joseph, Far be it from our lord to speak thus, for Your servants are twelve brothers, the sons of one man, our father Jacob, in the land of Canaan, the son of Isaac, the son of Abraham, the Hebrew, and, behold, the youngest is this day with our father in the land of Canaan, and one is not, for he was lost from us, and we thought perhaps he might be in this land, so we are seeking him throughout the land, and have come even to the houses of harlots to seek him there.

(Jasher 51:27)
And Joseph said to them, And have you then sought him throughout the earth, that there only remained Egypt for you to seek him in? And what also should your brother do in the houses of harlots, although he were in Egypt? Have you not said, That you are from the sons of Isaac, the son of Abraham, and what shall the sons of Jacob do then in the houses of harlots?

(Jasher 51:28)
And they said to him, Because we heard that Ishmaelites stole him from us, and it was told to us that they sold him in Egypt, and your servant, our brother, is very comely and well favored, so we thought he would surely be in the houses of harlots, therefore your servants went there to seek him and give ransom for him.

(Jasher 51:29)
And Joseph still answered them, saying, Surely you speak falsely and utter lies, to say of yourselves that you are the sons of Abraham; as Pharaoh lives you are spies, therefore have you come to the houses of harlots that you should not be known.

(Jasher 51:30)
And Joseph said to them, And now if you find him, and his master requires of you a great price, will you give it for him? And they said, It shall be given.

(Jasher 51:31)
And he said to them, And if his master will not consent to part with him for a great price, what will you do to him on his account? And they answered him, saying, If he will not give him to us we will slay him, and take our brother and go away.

(Genesis 42:14) (Jasher 51:32)
And Joseph said to them, It is as I spoke to you, saying, You are spies, for you are come to slay the inhabitants of the land, for we heard that two of your brothers smote all the inhabitants of Shechem, in the land of Canaan, on account of your sister, and you now come to do the like in Egypt on account of your brother.

(Genesis 42:15) (Jasher 51:33...)
Only hereby shall I know that you are true men and you shall be proved: By the life of Pharaoh you shall not go forth from here, except your youngest brother come here.

(Genesis 42:16) (...Jasher 51:33)
If you will send one of you, and let him fetch your youngest brother from your father, and to bring him here to me, and by

doing this thing I will know that you are right. And you shall be kept in prison, that your words may be proved, whether there be any truth in you: or else by the life of Pharaoh surely you are spies.

(Jasher 51:34)
And Joseph called to seventy of his mighty men, and he said to them, Take these men and bring them into the ward.

(Genesis 42:17) (Jasher 51:35) (...Jubilees 42:5)
And the mighty men took the ten men, they laid hold of them and he put them all together into ward and they were in the ward three days.

(Genesis 42:18) (Jasher 51:36...)
And Joseph had them brought out of the ward, and he said to them the third day, Do this for yourselves, and live; for I fear God:

(Genesis 42:19) (...Jasher 51:36...)
If you be true men, let one of your brothers be bound in the house of your prison: while you go, carry corn for the famine of your houses to the land of Canaan:

(Genesis 42:20) (...Jasher 51:36) (Jubilees 42:8)
And he commanded them: But fetch and bring your youngest brother here to me; so your words shall be verified. I may know that you are true men when you do this thing. And you shall not die; for they had told him their father was living and their younger brother. And they did so.

(Genesis 42:21)
And they said one to another, We are verily guilty concerning our brother, in that we saw the anguish of his soul, when he

besought us, and we would not hear; therefore this distress has come on us.

(Genesis 42:22)

And Reuben answered them, saying, Didn't I speak to you, saying, Do not sin against the child; but you would not hear? Therefore, behold, also his blood is required.

(Genesis 42:23)

And they did not know that Joseph understood them; for he spoke to them by an interpreter.

(Genesis 42:24...) (Jasher 51:37) (Jubilees 42:6)

And he turned himself about and went out from them and came into the chamber, and wept a great weeping, for his pity was excited for them, and he washed his face, and returned to them again, and communed with them. And after that he set them free again, and he took from them Simeon alone, and ordered him to be bound, but Simeon was not willing to be done so, for he was a very powerful man and they could not bind him.

(Jasher 51:38)

And Joseph called to his mighty men and seventy valiant men came before him with drawn swords in their hands, and the sons of Jacob were terrified at them.

(Jasher 51:39)

And Joseph said to them, Seize this man and confine him in prison until his brothers come to him, and Joseph's valiant men hastened and they all laid hold of Simeon to bind him, and Simeon gave a loud and terrible shriek and the cry was heard at a distance.

(Jasher 51:40)
And all the valiant men of Joseph were terrified at the sound of the shriek, that they fell upon their faces, and they were greatly afraid and fled.

(Jasher 51:41)
And all the men that were with Joseph fled, for they were greatly afraid of their lives, and only Joseph and Manasseh his son remained there, and Manassah the son of Joseph saw the strength of Simeon, and he was exceedingly wroth.

(Jasher 51:42)
And Manassah the son of Joseph rose up to Simeon, and Manassah smote Simeon a heavy blow with his fist against the back of his neck, and Simeon was stilled of his rage.

(...Genesis 42:24) (Jasher 51:43) (Jubilees 42:6...)
And Manassah laid hold of Simeon and he seized him violently and he bound him before their eyes and brought him into the house of confinement, and all the sons of Jacob were astonished at the act of the youth.

(Jasher 51:44)
And Simeon said to his brothers, None of you must say that this is the smiting of an Egyptian, but it is the smiting of the house of my father.

(Genesis 42:25) (Jasher 51:45) (Jubilees 42:7)
And then after this Joseph ordered him to be called who was set over the storehouse and commanded him to fill their sacks with corn, as much as they could carry, and to restore every man's money into his sack, and to give them provision for the way: and thus he did to them and they did not know.

(Jasher 51:46)
And Joseph commanded them, saying, Take heed lest you transgress my orders to bring your brother as I have told you, and it shall be when you bring your brother here to me, then will I know that you are true men, and you shall traffic in the land, and I will restore to you your brother, and you shall return in peace to your father.

(Jasher 51:47)
And they all answered and said, According as our lord speaks, so will we do, and they bowed down to him to the ground.

(Genesis 42:26) (Jasher 51:48...) (...Jubilees 42:6)
And every man loaded their donkeys with the corn, and Joseph sent off his nine brothers, and they departed there and they went out to go to the land of Canaan to their father.

(Genesis 42:27) (...Jasher 51:48)
And as one of them - Levi opened his sack to give his donkey provender in the inn, he espied his money in full weight; for, behold, it was still in his sack's mouth.

(Genesis 42:28) (Jasher 51:49)
And the man was greatly afraid, and he said to his brothers, My money has been restored; and, lo, it is even in my sack: and their heart failed them, and they were greatly afraid, saying one to another, What is this that God has done to us?

(Jasher 51:50)
And they all said, And where is the Lord's kindness with our fathers, with Abraham, Isaac, end Jacob, that the Lord has this day delivered us into the hands of the king of Egypt to contrive against us?

(Jasher 51:51)
And Judah said to them, Surely we are guilty sinners before the Lord our God in having sold our brother, our own flesh, and wherefore do you say, Where is the Lord's kindness with our fathers?

(Jasher 51:52)
And Reuben said to them, Did I not say to you, do not sin against the lad, and you would not listen to me? Now God requires him from us, and how dare you say, Where is the Lord's kindness with our fathers, while you have sinned to the Lord?

(Genesis 42:29...) (Jasher 51:53) (Jubilees 42:9...)
And they tarried overnight in that place, and they rose up early in the morning and laded their donkeys with their corn, and they led them and they went on up from the land of Egypt and they came to Jacob their father to the land of Canaan.

(...Genesis 42:29) (Jasher 51:54) (Jubilees 42:9...)
And Jacob and his household went out to meet his sons, and Jacob saw and behold their brother Simeon was not with them, and Jacob said to his sons, Where is your brother Simeon, whom I do not see? And his sons told him all that befell to them in Egypt; saying,

(Genesis 42:30) (...Jubilees 42:9...)
The man, who is the lord of the land, spoke roughly to us, and took us for spies of the country.

(Genesis 42:31)
And we said to him, We are true men; we are not spies:

(Genesis 42:32)

We be twelve brothers, sons of our father; one is not, and the youngest is this day with our father in the land of Canaan.

(Genesis 42:33)

And the man, the lord of the country, said to us, Hereby shall I know that you are true men; leave one of your brothers here with me, and take food for the famine of your households, and be gone:

(Genesis 42:34) (...Jubilees 42:9)

And bring your youngest brother to me: then I shall know that you are not spies, but that you are true men: so I will deliver you your brother, and you shall trade in the land.

(Genesis 42:35) (Jasher 52:1)

And they entered their house. And it came to pass as every man opened and emptied their sacks, that, they saw behold, every man's bundle of money was there, in his sack: and when both they and their father saw the bundles of money, they were greatly afraid.

(Genesis 42:36) (Jasher 52:2, 3) (Jubilees 42:10)

And Jacob their father said to them, What is this that you have done to me? You have bereaved me of my children: I sent your brother Joseph to inquire after your welfare and you said to me. A wild beast devoured him, now Joseph is not. And Simeon went with you to buy food and you say the king of Egypt hath confined him in prison, and Simeon is not, and you will take Benjamin away to cause his death also, and bring down my gray hairs with sorrow to the grave on account of Benjamin and his brother Joseph: all these things are against me. On me has your wickedness come.

(Genesis 42:37) (Jasher 52:5)

And Reuben spoke to his father, saying, You shall slay my two sons, if I do not bring him and place him before you: deliver him into my hand, and I will bring him to you again. And Jacob said to his sons, Abide here and do not go down to Egypt, for my son shall not go down with you to Egypt, nor die like his brother.

(Genesis 42:38) (Jasher 52:4) (Jubilees 42:11)

And he said, My son shall not go down with you lest perchance he fall sick; for their mother gave birth to two sons, and his brother is dead, and he is left alone: and this one also you will take from me. If mischief befall him by the way in the which you go, as it befell his brother, or if perchance he took a fever on the road, then shall you bring down my gray hairs with sorrow to the grave.

(Jubilees 42:12)

For he saw that their money had been returned to every man in his sack, and for this reason he feared to send him.

(Jasher 52:6)

And Judah said to them, refrain ye from him until the corn is finished, and he will then say, Take down your brother, when he will find his own life and the life of his household in danger from the famine.

Genesis: Chapter Forty-Three

(Genesis 43:1) (Jasher 52:7...) (Jubilees 42:13)

And in those days the famine increased and was sore in the land of Canaan, and in all lands, save in the land of Egypt, for many of the children of the Egyptians had stored up their seed for food from the time when they saw Joseph gathering seed together and putting it in storehouses and preserving it for the years of famine.

(Jubilees 42:14)

And the people of Egypt fed themselves on it during the first year of their famine.

(...Jasher 52:7)

And all the people of the earth went and came to Egypt to buy food, for the famine prevailed greatly among them, and the sons of Jacob remained in Canaan a year and two months until their corn was finished.

(Genesis 43:2) (Jasher 52:8)

And it came to pass, when they had eaten up the corn which they had brought out of Egypt, the whole household of Jacob was pinched with hunger, and all the infants of the sons of Jacob came together and they approached Jacob, and they all surrounded him, and they said to him, Give to us bread, and wherefore shall we all perish through hunger in your presence?

(Jasher 52:9)

Jacob heard the words of his son's children, and he wept a great weeping, and his pity was roused for them, and Jacob called to his sons and they all came and sat before him.

(Genesis 43:2) (Jasher 52:10) (Jubilees 42:15)

But when Israel saw that the famine was very sore in the land, and that there was no deliverance: Jacob, their father said to them, And have you not seen how your children have been weeping over me this day, saying, Give to us bread, and there is none? Now therefore Go again, buy us a little food that we die not.

(Jubilees 42:16)

And they said: We shall not go; unless our youngest brother go with us, we shall not go.

(Genesis 43:3) (Jasher 52:11...)

And Judah spoke to his father, saying, The man solemnly protested to us, saying, You shall not see my face, except your brother be with you.

(Genesis 43:4) (...Jasher 52:11...)

If you will send our brother with us, we will go down and buy food for you:

(Genesis 43:5) (...Jasher 52:11)

But if you will not send him, we will not go down: for the man - the king of Egypt particularly said to us, You shall not see my face, except your brother be with you for the king of Egypt is a strong and mighty king, and behold if we shall go to him without our brother we shall all be put to death.

(Genesis 43:6) (Jasher 52:18...)

And Israel said, Why did you deal so ill with me, as to tell the man whether you had yet a brother?

(Jasher 52:12)
And Judah said Do you not know and have you not heard that this king is very powerful and wise, and there is not like to him in all the earth? Behold we have seen all the kings of the earth and we have not seen one like that king, the king of Egypt; surely among all the kings of the earth there is none greater than Abimelech king of the Philistines, yet the king of Egypt is greater and mightier than he, and Abimelech can only be compared to one of his officers.

(Jasher 52:13)
Father, you have not seen his palace and his throne, and all his servants standing before him; you have not seen that king upon his throne in his pomp and royal appearance, dressed in his kingly robes with a large golden crown upon his head; you have not seen the honor and glory which God has given to him, for there is not like to him in all the earth.

(Jasher 52:14)
Father, you have not seen the wisdom, the understanding and the knowledge which God has given in his heart, nor heard his sweet voice when he spoke to us.

(Genesis 43:7) (Jasher 52:15)
And they said, We know not, father, who made him acquainted with our names and all that befell us, yet the man asked us strait up of our state, and of our kindred, he asked also after you saying, Is your father yet alive? And is it well with him? Have you another brother? And we told him according to the tenor of these words: could we certainly know that he would say, Bring your brother down?

(Jasher 52:16)
You have not seen the affairs of the government of Egypt regulated by him, without inquiring of Pharaoh his lord; you

have not seen the awe and fear which he impressed upon all the Egyptians.

(Jasher 52:17)
And also when we went from him, we threatened to do to Egypt like to the rest of the cities of the Amorites, and we were exceedingly wroth against all his words which he spoke concerning us as spies, and now when we shall again come before him his terror will fall upon us all, and not one of us will be able to speak to him either a little or a great thing.

(Genesis 43:8) (...Jasher 52:18)
And Judah said to Israel his father, Now therefore father, send, we pray, the lad with me, and we will arise and go down and buy you food for our support, that we may live, and not die through hunger, both we, and you, and also our little ones.

(Jubilees 42:17)
And Israel saw that if he did not send him with them, they should all perish by reason of the famine

(Jubilees 42:18)
And Reuben said: Give him into my hand, and if I do not bring him back to you, slay my two sons instead of his soul.

(Genesis 43:9) (Jasher 52:19) (Jubilees 42:19)
And he said to him: He shall not go with you. And Judah came near and said to Jacob his father, Give the lad into my care, send him with me and we will rise up and go down to Egypt and buy corn, and then return, I will be surety for him; of my hand shall you require him: and it shall be when we return if the lad be not with us, if I bring him not to you, and set him before you, then let me bear the blame before you forever:

(Jasher 52:20)
Have you seen all our infants weeping over you through hunger and there is no power in your hand to satisfy them? Now let your pity be roused for them and send our brother with us and we will go

(Genesis 43:10) (Jasher 52:21)
For how will the Lord's kindness to our ancestors be manifested to you when you say that the king of Egypt will take away your son? As the Lord lives I will not leave him until I bring him and place him before you; but pray for us to the Lord, that he may deal kindly with us, to cause us to be received favorably and kindly before the king of Egypt and his men, for except we had lingered, surely now we had returned this second time with your son.

(Jasher 52:22)
And Jacob said to his sons, I trust in the Lord God that he may deliver you and give you favor in the sight of the king of Egypt, and in the sight of all his men.

(Genesis 43:11) (Jasher 52:23...)
And their father Israel said to them, If it must be so now, do this; take of the best fruits that can be obtained in the land in your vessels. Now therefore rise up and carry down a present to the man and bring it before him, a little balm, and a little honey, spices, and myrrh, nuts, and almonds:

(Genesis 43:12)
And take double money in your hand; and the money that was brought again in the mouth of your sacks, carry it again in your hand; peradventure it was an oversight:

(Genesis 43:13)

Take also your brother, and arise, go again to the man:

(Genesis 43:14) (...Jasher 52:23)

And God Almighty give you mercy before the man, that he may send away your other brother, and Benjamin with you. If I be bereaved of my children, I am bereaved.

(Jubilees 42:20...)

And he sent him with them in the second year of this week on the first day of the month,

(Genesis 43:15...) (Jasher 52:24)

And all the men took that large present of the best of the land, and they took double money in their hand, and their brother Benjamin; and rose up.

(Jasher 52:25)

And Jacob strictly commanded his sons concerning Benjamin, Saying, Take heed of him in the way in which you are going, and do not separate yourselves from him in the road, neither in Egypt.

(Jasher 52:26)

And Jacob rose up from his sons and spread forth his hands and he prayed to the Lord on account of his sons, saying, O Lord God of heaven and earth, remember your covenant with our father Abraham, remember it with my father Isaac and deal kindly with my sons and deliver them not into the hands of the king of Egypt; do it I pray you O God for the sake of your mercies and redeem all my children and rescue them from Egyptian power, and send them their two brothers.

(Jasher 52:27)
And all the wives of the sons of Jacob and their children lifted up their eyes to heaven and they all wept before the Lord, and cried to him to deliver their fathers from the hand of the king of Egypt.

(Jasher 52:28)
And Jacob wrote a record to the king of Egypt and gave it into the hand of Judah and into the hands of his sons for the king of Egypt, saying,

(Jasher 52:29)
From your servant Jacob, son of Isaac, son of Abraham the Hebrew, the prince of God, to the powerful and wise king, the revealer of secrets, king of Egypt, greeting.

(Jasher 52:30)
Be it known to my lord the king of Egypt, the famine was sore upon us in the land of Canaan, and I sent my sons to you to buy us a little food from you for our support.

(Jasher 52:31)
For my sons surrounded me and I being very old cannot see with my eyes, for my eyes have become very heavy through age, as well as with daily weeping for my son, for Joseph who was lost from before me, and I commanded my sons that they should not enter the gates of the city when they came to Egypt, on account of the inhabitants of the land.

(Jasher 52:32)
And I also commanded them to go about Egypt to seek for my son Joseph, perhaps they might find him there, and they did so, and you considered them as spies of the land.

(Jasher 52:33)
Have we not heard concerning you that you interpreted Pharaoh's dream and spoke truly to him? How then do you not know in your wisdom whether my sons are spies or not?

(Jasher 52:34)
Now therefore, my lord and king, behold I have sent my son before you, as you spoke to my sons; I beseech you to put your eyes upon him until he is returned to me in peace with his brothers.

(Jasher 52:35)
For do you not know, or have you not heard that which our God did to Pharaoh when he took my mother Sarah, and what he did to Abimelech king of the Philistines on account of her, and also what our father Abraham did to the nine kings of Elam, how he smote them all with a few men that were with him?

(Jasher 52:36)
And also, what my two sons Simeon and Levi did to the eight cities of the Amorites, how they destroyed them on account of their sister Dinah?

(Jasher 52:37)
And also on account of their brother Benjamin they consoled themselves for the loss of his brother Joseph; what will they then do for him when they see the hand of any people prevailing over them, for his sake?

(Jasher 52:38)
Do you not know, O king of Egypt, that the power of God is with us, and that also God ever hears our prayers and does not forsake us all the days?

(Jasher 52:39)
And when my sons told me of your dealings with them, I called not to the Lord on account of you, for then you wouldst have perished with your men before my son Benjamin came before you, but I thought that as Simeon my son was in your house, perhaps you might deal kindly with him, therefore I did not this thing to you.

(Jasher 52:40)
Now therefore behold Benjamin my son comes to you with my sons, take heed of him and put your eyes upon him, and then will God place his eyes over you and throughout your kingdom.

(Jasher 52:41)
Now I have told you all that is in my heart, and behold my sons are coming to you with their brother, examine the face of the whole earth for their sake and send them back in peace with their brothers.

(Jasher 52:42)
And Jacob gave the record to his sons into the care of Judah to give it to the king of Egypt.

(...Genesis 43:15) (Jasher 53:1) (...Jubilees 42:20, 21...)
And the sons of Jacob rose up, and took Benjamin. And they came to the land of Egypt with all those who went, and they had all of the presents in their hands, stacte and almonds and terebinth nuts and pure honey. And they went down to Egypt, and they stood before Joseph.

(Genesis 43:16) (Jasher 53:2...) (Jubilees 42:22...)
And when Joseph saw his brother Benjamin with them, and he saluted them. He said to the ruler of his house, Bring these

men home, and slay, and make ready; for these men shall dine with me at noon; and he sent him into his house.

(Genesis 43:17) (...Jasher 53:2)
And the man did as Joseph commanded; and the man brought the men into Joseph's house.

(Jasher 53:3)
And Joseph commanded the superintendent of his house to give to his brothers to eat, and he did so to them.

(Genesis 43:18)
And the men were afraid, because they were brought into Joseph's house; and they said, Because of the money that was returned in our sacks at the first time are we brought in; that he may seek occasion against us, and fall on us, and take us for bondmen, and our donkeys.

(Genesis 43:19)
And they came near to the steward of Joseph's house, and they communed with him at the door of the house,

(Jasher 53:4...)
And the men told the superintendent of Joseph's house concerning the silver that was returned in their sacks,

(Genesis 43:20)
And said, O sir, we came indeed down at the first time to buy food:

(Genesis 43:21)
And it came to pass, when we came to the inn, that we opened our sacks, and, behold, every man's money was in the mouth of his sack, our money in full weight: and we have brought it

again in our hand.

(Genesis 43:22)
And other money have we brought down in our hands to buy food: we cannot tell who put our money in our sacks.

(Genesis 43:23) (...Jasher 53:4...) (...Jubilees 42:22...)
And he said to them, Peace be to you, fear not: your God, and the God of your father, has given you treasure in your sacks: I had your money. And he brought Simeon out to them.

(Jasher 53:5)
And Simeon said to his brothers, The lord of the Egyptians has acted very kindly to me, he did not keep me bound, as you saw with your eyes, for when you went out from the city he let me free and dealt kindly with me in his house.

(Genesis 43:24)
And the man brought the men into Joseph's house, and gave them water, and they washed their feet; and he gave their donkeys provender.

(Genesis 43:25)
And they made ready the present against Joseph came at noon: for they heard that they should eat bread there.

(Genesis 43:26...) (...Jasher 53:4) (...Jubilees 42:22...)
And at noon time when Joseph came home, he made a feast for them, and he sent for the men to come before him with Benjamin.

(...Genesis 43:26) (Jasher 53:6, 7...) (...Jubilees 42:22)
And Judah took Benjamin by the hand, and they came before Joseph, And the men brought him the present which was in

their hand into the house, and bowed themselves to him to the earth.

(Genesis 43:27) (...Jasher 53:7...)
And they all sat before him, and Joseph asked them of their welfare, and said, Is it well with you, is it well with your children? Is your aged father well, the old man of whom you spoke? Is he yet alive?

(Genesis 43:28) (...Jasher 53:7)
And they answered, It is well. Your servant our father is in good health, he is yet alive. And they bowed down their heads, and made obeisance. And Judah took the record which Jacob had sent and gave it into the hand of Joseph.

(Jasher 53:8)
And Joseph read the letter and knew his father's writing, and he wished to weep and he went into an inner room and he wept a great weeping; and he went out.

(Genesis 43:29) (Jasher 53:9) (...Jubilees 42:21)
And he lifted up his eyes, and saw his brother Benjamin, his mother's son, and he knew him, and said, Is this your younger brother, of whom you spoke to me? And they said to him: It is he. And Benjamin approached Joseph, and Joseph placed his hand upon his head and he said to him, God be gracious to you, my son.

(Genesis 43:30) (Jasher 53:10...)
And when Joseph saw his brother, the son of his mother, he again wished to weep, and he made haste; for his bowels yearned on his brother: and he sought where to weep; and he entered into his chamber, and wept there.

(Genesis 43:31) (...Jasher 53:10)

And he washed his face, and went out, and refrained himself from weeping, and said, Set on bread.

(Genesis 43:32)

And they set on for him by himself, and for them by themselves, and for the Egyptians, which ate with him, by themselves: because the Egyptians might not eat bread with the Hebrews; for that is an abomination to the Egyptians.

(Jasher 53:11)

And Joseph had a cup from which he drank, and it was of silver beautifully inlaid with onyx stones and bdellium, and Joseph struck the cup in the sight of his brothers while they were sitting to eat with him.

(Jasher 53:12)

And Joseph said to the men, I know by this cup that Reuben the first born, Simeon and Levi and Judah, Issachar and Zebulun are children from one mother, seat yourselves to eat according to your births.

(Jasher 53:13)

And he also placed the others according to their births, and he said, I know that this your youngest brother has no brother, and I, like him, have no brother, he shall therefore sit down to eat with me.

(Genesis 43:33) (Jasher 53:14...)

And they sat before him, the firstborn according to his birthright, and the youngest according to his youth: And Benjamin went up before Joseph and sat upon the throne, and the men beheld the acts of Joseph, and they were astonished at them and marveled one at another.

(Genesis 43:34...) (...Jasher 53:14) (Jubilees 42:23, 24...)
And he took and sent messes to them and they ate from before him: but Benjamin's mess was five times so much as any of theirs. And they drank at that time with Joseph. And he then gave presents to them, and Joseph gave one gift to Benjamin, and Manasseh and Ephraim saw the acts of their father, and they also gave presents to him, and Osnath gave him one present, and they were five presents in the hand of Benjamin.

(Jasher 53:15)
And Joseph brought them out wine to drink, and they would not drink, and they said, From the day on which Joseph was lost we have not drunk wine, nor eaten any delicacies.

(...Genesis 43:34) (Jasher 53:16)
And Joseph swore to them, and he pressed them hard, and they drank plentifully with him on that day, and were merry with him. And Joseph afterward turned to his brother Benjamin to speak with him, and Benjamin was still sitting upon the throne before Joseph.

(Jasher 53:17)
And Joseph said to him, Have you begotten any children? And he said, Your servant has ten sons, and these are their names, Bela, Becher, Ashbal, Gera, Naaman, Achi, Rosh, Mupim, Chupim, and Ord, and I called their names after my brother whom I have not seen.

(Jasher 53:18)
And he ordered them to bring before him his map of the stars, whereby Joseph knew all the times, and Joseph said to Benjamin, I have heard that the Hebrews are acquainted with all wisdom, do you know anything of this?

(Jasher 53:19)
And Benjamin said, Your servant is knowing also in all the wisdom which my father taught me, and Joseph said to Benjamin, Look now at this instrument and understand where your brother Joseph is in Egypt, who you said went down to Egypt.

(Jasher 53:20)
And Benjamin beheld that instrument with the map of the stars of heaven, and he was wise and looked therein to know where his brother was, and Benjamin divided the whole land of Egypt into four divisions, and he found that he who was sitting upon the throne before him was his brother Joseph, and Benjamin wondered greatly, and when Joseph saw that his brother Benjamin was so much astonished, he said to Benjamin, What have you seen, and why are you astonished?

(Jasher 53:21)
And Benjamin said to Joseph, I can see by this that Joseph my brother sits here with me upon the throne, and Joseph said to him, I am Joseph your brother, do not reveal this thing to your brothers; behold I will send you with them when they go away, and I will command them to be brought back again into the city, and I will take you away from them.

(Jasher 53:22)
And if they dare their lives and fight for you, then shall I know that they have repented of what they did to me, and I will make myself known to them, and if they forsake you when I take you, then shall you remain with me, and I will wrangle with them, and they shall go away, and I will not become known to them.

(...Jubilees 42:24)
And Joseph's brothers arose and remained with their donkeys.

Genesis: Chapter Forty-Four

(Genesis 44:1) (Jasher 53:23...) (Jubilees 42:25...)
And at that time Joseph devised a plan whereby he might learn their thoughts as to whether thoughts of peace prevailed among them, and he commanded his officer, the steward of his house, saying, Fill the men's sacks with food, as much as they can carry, and put every man's money in his sack's mouth.

(Genesis 44:2) (...Jasher 53:23) (...Jubilees 42:25)
And put my cup, the silver cup out of which I drink, in the sack's mouth of Benjamin, the youngest, and his corn money. And give them provision for the road and send them away.

(Genesis 44:2) (...Jasher 53:23) (Jubilees 43:1)
And he did so to them according to the word that Joseph had spoken, and filled all their sacks for them with food and put their money in their sacks, and put the cup in Benjamin's sack.

(Genesis 44:3) (Jasher 53:24) (Jubilees 43:2...)
And on the next day, as soon as the morning was light, the men rose up and they loaded their donkeys with their corn, and were sent away, they and their donkeys. And they went forth with Benjamin, and they went to the land of Canaan with their brother Benjamin.

(Genesis 44:4) (Jasher 53:25) (...Jubilees 43:2...)
And it came to pass that, when they were gone out of the city, and not yet far off from Egypt, when Joseph said to his steward that was set over his house, saying, Rise up, follow after the men before they get too far from Egypt; run and

seize them, and when you overtake them, say to them, Why have you rewarded evil for good? Why have you stolen from me my master's cup?

(Genesis 44:5) (...Jubilees 43:2)
Is not this the silver cup out of in which my lord drinks, and whereby indeed he divines? You have done evil in so doing. And bring back to me their youngest brother, and fetch him quickly before I go forth to my seat of judgment.

(Genesis 44:6) (Jasher 53:26...) (Jubilees 43:3)
And Joseph's officer rose up and he ran after them. And he overtook them, and he spoke to them these same words, all the words of Joseph.

(Genesis 44:7) (...Jasher 53:26) (Jubilees 43:4)
And when they heard this thing they became exceedingly wroth, and they said to him, Why does my lord say these words? God forbid that your servants should do according to this thing: and steal from the house of your lord any utensil, and the money also which we found in our sacks the first time, we your servants brought back from the land of Canaan.

(Genesis 44:8) (Jubilees 43:5...)
Behold, the money, which we found in our sacks' mouths, we brought again to you out of the land of Canaan: how then should we steal out of your lord's house any utensil, silver or gold?

(Genesis 44:9) (...Jasher 53:26) (...Jubilees 43:5)
Behold here are we and our sacks search, and with whomsoever of your servants your master's cup be found in the sack of any man among us, both let him die, and we and our donkeys also will be my lord's bondmen.

(Genesis 44:10) (Jubilees 43:6)
And he said, Not so. Now also let it be according to your words, he with whom it is found shall be my servant; and you shall be blameless, you shall return in peace to your house.

(Genesis 44:11) (Jasher 53:27...)
Then they speedily took down every man his sack from his donkey to the ground, and opened every man his sack and they looked in their bags.

(Genesis 44:12) (...Jasher 53:27...) (Jubilees 43:7)
And he searched, and began at the eldest, and left at the youngest: and the cup was found in Benjamin's sack.

(Genesis 44:13) (...Jasher 53:27) (Jubilees 43:8...)
Then they rent their clothes, and laded every man his donkey, and returned to the city. And they smote Benjamin in the road, continually smiting him until he came into the city, and they stood before Joseph.

(Jasher 53:28)
And Judah's anger was kindled, and he said, This man has only brought me back to destroy Egypt this day.

(Genesis 44:14) (Jasher 53:29) (...Jubilees 43:8)
And Judah and his brothers came to Joseph's house: and they found Joseph sitting upon his throne, for he was yet there, and all the mighty men standing at his right and left. And they fell before him on the ground.

(Genesis 44:15) (Jasher 53:30) (Jubilees 43:9...)
And Joseph said to them, What deed is this that you have done? You have done evil, that you took away my silver cup and went away? But I know that you took my cup in order to

know thereby in what part of the land your brother was. Do you not know that such a man as I can certainly divine?

(Genesis 44:16) (Jasher 53:31) (...Jubilees 43:9)

And Judah said, What shall we say to my lord? What shall we speak? Or how shall we clear ourselves? God has this day found out the iniquity of your servants, therefore has he done this thing to us this day. Behold, we are my lord's servants, both we, and he also with whom the cup is found, and our donkeys also.

(Genesis 44:17) (Jubilees 43:10)

And he said to them, God forbid that I should do so for I too fear the Lord: but let your brother, the man in whose hand the cup is found, he shall be my servant; for you have done evil. Know you not that a man delights in his cup as I with this cup? And yet you have stolen it from me. And as for you, go to your homes, get up in peace to your father.

(Genesis 44:18) (Jubilees 43:11...)

Then Judah came near to him, and said Oh my lord, let your servant, I pray, speak a word in my lord's ears, and let not your anger burn against your servant: for you are even as Pharaoh.

(Genesis 44:19)

My lord asked his servants, saying, Have you a father, or a brother?

(Genesis 44:20) (...Jubilees 43:11)

And we said to my lord, We have a father, an old man, and a child of his old age, a little one; two brothers did your servant's mother bear to our father: one went away and was lost, and has not been found, his brother is dead, and he alone is left of his mother, and your servant his father loves him and his life also is bound up with the life of this (lad).

(Genesis 44:21)
And you said to your servants, Bring him down to me, that I may set my eyes on him.

(Genesis 44:22)
And we said to my lord, The lad cannot leave his father: for if he should leave his father, his father would die.

(Genesis 44:23)
And you said to your servants, Except your youngest brother come down with you, you shall see my face no more.

(Genesis 44:24)
And it came to pass when we came up to your servant my father, we told him the words of my lord.

(Genesis 44:25)
And our father said, Go again, and buy us a little food.

(Genesis 44:26)
And we said, We cannot go down: if our youngest brother be with us, then will we go down: for we may not see the man's face, except our youngest brother be with us.

(Genesis 44:27)
And your servant my father said to us, You know that my wife bore me two sons:

(Genesis 44:28)
And the one went out from me, and I said, Surely he is torn in pieces; and I saw him not since:

(Genesis 44:29)

And if you take this also from me, and mischief befall him, you shall bring down my gray hairs with sorrow to the grave.

(Genesis 44:30)

Now therefore when I come to your servant my father, and the lad be not with us; seeing that his life is bound up in the lad's life;

(Genesis 44:31) (Jubilees 43:12)

It shall come to pass, when we go to your servant our father, and he sees that the lad is not with us, that he will die: and your servants shall bring down the gray hairs of your servant our father with sorrow to the grave.

(Genesis 44:32) (Jubilees 43:13...)

For your servant became surety for the lad to my father, saying, If I bring him not to you, then I shall bear the blame to my father forever.

(Genesis 44:33) (...Jubilees 43:13)

Now therefore, I pray, let your servant abide instead of the lad a bondman to my lord; and let the lad go up with his brothers.

(Genesis 44:34)

For how shall I go up to my father, and the lad be not with me? Lest peradventure I see the evil that shall come on my father.

(Jasher 53:32)

And Joseph rose up and caught hold of Benjamin and took him from his brothers with violence, and he came to the house and locked the door at them, and Joseph commanded him that was set over his house that he should say to them, Thus says the king, Go in peace to your father, behold I have taken the man in whose hand my cup was found.

~ ~ ~

(Jasher 54:1)
And when Judah saw the dealings of Joseph with them, Judah approached him and broke open the door, and came with his brothers before Joseph.

(Jasher 54:2)
And Judah said to Joseph, Let it not seem grievous in the sight of my lord, may your servant I pray you speak a word before you? And Joseph said to him, Speak.

(Jasher 54:3)
And Judah spoke before Joseph, and his brothers were there standing before them; and Judah said to Joseph, Surely when we first came to our lord to buy food, you considered us as spies of the land, and we brought Benjamin before you, and you still make sport of us this day.

(Jasher 54:4)
Now therefore let the king hear my words, and send I pray you our brother that he may go along with us to our father, lest your soul perish this day with all the souls of the inhabitants of Egypt.

(Jasher 54:5)
Do you not know what two of my brothers, Simeon and Levi, did to the city of Shechem, and to seven cities of the Amorites, on account of our sister Dinah, and also what they would do

for the sake of their brother Benjamin?

(Jasher 54:6)
And I with my strength, who am greater and mightier than both of them, come this day upon you and your land if you are unwilling to send our brother.

(Jasher 54:7)
Have you not heard what our God who made choice of us did to Pharaoh on account of Sarah our mother, whom he took away from our father, that he smote him and his household with heavy plagues, that even to this day the Egyptians relate this wonder to each other? So will our God do to you on account of Benjamin whom you have this day taken from his father, and on account of the evils which you this day heaps over us in your land; for our God will remember his covenant with our father Abraham and bring evil upon you, because you have grieved the soul of our father this day.

(Jasher 54:8)
Now therefore hear my words that I have this day spoken to you, and send our brother that he may go away lest you and the people of your land die by the sword, for you cannot all prevail over me.

(Jasher 54:9)
And Joseph answered Judah, saying, Why have you opened wide your mouth and why do you boast over us, saying, Strength is with you? As Pharaoh lives, if I command all my valiant men to fight with you, surely you and these your brothers would sink in the mire.

(Jasher 54:10)
And Judah said to Joseph, Surely it becomes you and your

people to fear me; as the Lord lives if I once draw my sword I shall not sheathe it again until I shall this day have slain all Egypt, and I will commence with you and finish with Pharaoh your master.

(Jasher 54:11)
And Joseph answered and said to him, Surely strength belongs not alone to you; I am stronger and mightier than you, surely if you draw your sword I will put it to your neck and the necks of all your brothers.

(Jasher 54:12)
And Judah said to him, Surely if I this day open my mouth against you I would swallow you up that you be destroyed from off the earth and perish this day from your kingdom. And Joseph said, Surely if you open your mouth I have power and might to close your mouth with a stone until you shall not be able to utter a word; see how many stones are before us, truly I can take a stone, and force it into your mouth and break your jaws.

(Jasher 54:13)
And Judah said, God is witness between us, that we have not hitherto desired to battle with you, only give us our brother and we will go from you; and Joseph answered and said, As Pharaoh lives, if all the kings of Canaan came together with you, you should not take him from my hand.

(Jasher 54:14)
Now therefore go your way to your father, and your brother shall be to me for a slave, for he has robbed the king's house. And Judah said, What is it to you or to the character of the king, surely the king sends forth from his house, throughout the land, silver and gold either in gifts or expenses, and you

still talk about your cup which you placed in our brother's bag and say that he has stolen it from you?

(Jasher 54:15)
God forbid that our brother Benjamin or any of the seed of Abraham should do this thing to steal from you, or from anyone else, whether king, prince, or any man.

(Jasher 54:16)
Now therefore cease this accusation lest the whole earth hear your words, saying, For a little silver the king of Egypt wrangled with the men, and he accused them and took their brother for a slave.

(Jasher 54:17)
And Joseph answered and said, Take to you this cup and go from me and leave your brother for a slave, for it is the judgment of a thief to be a slave.

(Jasher 54:18)
And Judah said, Why are you not ashamed of your words, to leave our brother and to take your cup? Surely if you give us your cup, or a thousand times as much, we will not leave our brother for the silver which is found in the hand of any man, that we will not die over him.

(Jasher 54:19)
And Joseph answered, And why did you forsake your brother and sell him for twenty pieces of silver to this day, and why then will you not do the same to this your brother?

(Jasher 54:20)
And Judah said, the Lord is witness between me and you that we do not desire your battles; now therefore give us our

brother and we will go from you without quarreling.

(Jasher 54:21)
And Joseph answered and said, If all the kings of the land should assemble they will not be able to take your brother from my hand; and Judah said, What shall we say to our father, when he sees that our brother does not come with us, and will grieve over him?

(Jasher 54:22)
And Joseph answered and said, This is the thing which you shall tell to your father, saying, The rope has gone after the bucket.

(Jasher 54:23)
And Judah said, Surely you are a king, and why do you speak these things, giving a false judgment? Woe to the king who is like to you.

(Jasher 54:24)
And Joseph answered and said, There is no false judgment in the word that I spoke on account of your brother Joseph, for all of you sold him to the Midianites for twenty pieces of silver, and you all denied it to your father and said to him, An evil beast has devoured him, Joseph has been torn to pieces.

(Jasher 54:25)
And Judah said, Behold the fire of Shem burns in my heart, now I will burn all your land with fire; and Joseph answered and said, Surely your sister-in-law Tamar, who killed your sons, extinguished the fire of Shechem.

(Jasher 54:26)
And Judah said, If I pluck out a single hair from my flesh, I

will fill all Egypt with its blood.

(Jasher 54:27)
And Joseph answered and said, Such is your custom to do as you did to your brother whom you sold, and you dipped his coat in blood and brought it to your father in order that he might say an evil beast devoured him and here is his blood.

(Jasher 54:28)
And when Judah heard this thing he was exceedingly wroth and his anger burned within him, and there was before him in that place a stone, the weight of which was about four hundred shekels, and Judah's anger was kindled and he took the stone in one hand and cast it to the heavens and caught it with his left hand.

(Jasher 54:29)
And he placed it afterward under his legs, and he sat upon it with all his strength and the stone was turned into dust from the force of Judah.

(Jasher 54:30)
And Joseph saw the act of Judah and he was very much afraid, but he commanded Manassah his son and he also did with another stone like to the act of Judah, and Judah said to his brothers, Let not any of you say, this man is an Egyptian, but by his doing this thing he is of our father's family.

(Jasher 54:31)
And Joseph said, Not to you only is strength given, for we are also powerful men, and why will you boast over us all? And Judah said to Joseph, Send, I pray, our brother and ruin not your country this day.

(Jasher 54:32)
And Joseph answered and said to them, Go and tell your father, an evil beast hath devoured him as you said concerning your brother Joseph.

(Jasher 54:33)
And Judah spoke to his brother Naphtali, and he said to him, Make haste, go now and number all the streets of Egypt and come and tell me; and Simeon said to him, Do not let this thing be a trouble to you; now I will go to the mount and take up one large stone from the mount and level it at every one in Egypt, and kill all that are in it.

(Jasher 54:34)
And Joseph heard all these words that his brothers spoke before him, and they did not know that Joseph understood them, for they imagined that he did not know how to speak Hebrew.

(Jasher 54:35)
And Joseph was greatly afraid at the words of his brothers lest they should destroy Egypt, and he commanded his son Manasseh, saying, Go now make haste and gather to me all the inhabitants of Egypt, and all the valiant men together, and let them come to me now upon horseback and on foot and with all sorts of musical instruments, and Manasseh went and did so.

(Jasher 54:36)
And Naphtali went as Judah had commanded him, for Naphtali was light-footed as one of the swift stags, and he would go upon the ears of corn and they would not break under him.

(Jasher 54:37)
And he went and numbered all the streets of Egypt, and found them to be twelve, and he came hastily and told Judah, and Judah said to his brothers, Hurry and put on every man his sword upon his loins and we will come over Egypt, and smite them all, and let not a remnant remain.

(Jasher 54:38)
And Judah said, Behold, I will destroy three of the streets with my strength, and you shall each destroy one street; and when Judah was speaking this thing, behold the inhabitants of Egypt and all the mighty men came toward them with all sorts of musical instruments and with loud shouting.

(Jasher 54:39)
And their number was five hundred cavalry and ten thousand infantry, and four hundred men who could fight without sword or spear, only with their hands and strength.

(Jasher 54:40)
And all the mighty men came with great storming and shouting, and they all surrounded the sons of Jacob and terrified them, and the ground quaked at the sound of their shouting.

(Jasher 54:41)
And when the sons of Jacob saw these troops they were greatly afraid of their lives, and Joseph did so in order to terrify the sons of Jacob to become tranquilized.

(Jasher 54:42)
And Judah, seeing some of his brothers terrified, said to them, Why are you afraid while the grace of God is with us? And when Judah saw all the people of Egypt surrounding

them at the command of Joseph to terrify them, only Joseph commanded them, saying, Do not touch any of them.

(Jasher 54:43)
Then Judah hastened and drew his sword, and uttered a loud and bitter scream, and he smote with his sword, and he sprang upon the ground and he still continued to shout against all the people.

(Jasher 54:44)
And when he did this thing the Lord caused the terror of Judah and his brothers to fall upon the valiant men and all the people that surrounded them.

(Jasher 54:45)
And they all fled at the sound of the shouting, and they were terrified and fell one upon the other, and many of them died as they fell, and they all fled from before Judah and his brothers and from before Joseph.

(Jasher 54:46)
And while they were fleeing, Judah and his brothers pursued them to the house of Pharaoh, and they all escaped, and Judah again sat before Joseph and roared at him like a lion, and gave a great and tremendous shriek at him.

(Jasher 54:47)
And the shriek was heard at a distance, and all the inhabitants of Succoth heard it, and all Egypt quaked at the sound of the shriek, and also the walls of Egypt and of the land of Goshen fell in from the shaking of the earth, and Pharaoh also fell from his throne upon the ground, and also all the pregnant women of Egypt and Goshen miscarried when they heard the noise of the shaking, for they were terribly afraid.

(Jasher 54:48)
And Pharaoh sent word, saying, What is this thing that has this day happened in the land of Egypt? And they came and told him all the things from beginning to end, and Pharaoh was alarmed and he wondered and was greatly afraid.

(Jasher 54:49)
And his fright increased when he heard all these things, and he sent to Joseph, saying, You have brought to me the Hebrews to destroy all Egypt; what will you do with that thievish slave? Send him away and let him go with his brothers, and let us not perish through their evil, even we, you and all Egypt.

(Jasher 54:50)
And if you do not desire to do this thing, cast off from you all my valuable things, and go with them to their land, if you delight in it, for they will this day destroy my whole country and slay all my people; even all the women of Egypt have miscarried through their screams; see what they have done merely by their shouting and speaking, moreover if they fight with the sword, they will destroy the land; now therefore choose that which you desire, whether me or the Hebrews, whether Egypt or the land of the Hebrews.

(Jasher 54:51)
And they came and told Joseph all the words of Pharaoh that he had said concerning him, and Joseph was greatly afraid at the words of Pharaoh and Judah and his brothers were still standing before Joseph indignant and enraged, and all the sons of Jacob roared at Joseph, like the roaring of the sea and its waves.

(Jasher 54:52)
And Joseph was greatly afraid of his brothers and on account of Pharaoh, and Joseph sought a pretext to make himself

known to his brothers, lest they should destroy all Egypt.

(Jasher 54:53)
And Joseph commanded his son Manasseh, and Manasseh went and approached Judah, and placed his hand upon his shoulder, and the anger of Judah was stilled.

(Jasher 54:54)
And Judah said to his brothers, Let no one of you say that this is the act of an Egyptian youth for this is the work of my father's house.

(Jasher 54:55)
And Joseph seeing and knowing that Judah's anger was stilled, he approached to speak to Judah in the language of mildness.

(Jasher 54:56)
And Joseph said to Judah, Surely you speak truth and have this day verified your assertions concerning your strength, and may your God who delights in you, increase your welfare; but tell me truly why from among all your brothers do you wrangle with me on account of the lad, as none of them have spoken one word to me concerning him.

(Jasher 54:57)
And Judah answered Joseph, saying, Surely you must know that I was security for the lad to his father, saying, If I brought him not to him I should bear his blame forever.

(Jasher 54:58)
Therefore, I have approached you from among all my brothers, for I saw that you were unwilling to suffer him to go from you; now therefore may I find grace in your sight that

you shall send him to go with us, and behold I will remain as a substitute for him, to serve you in whatever you desire, for wheresoever you shall send me I will go to serve you with great energy.

(Jasher 54:59)
Send me now to a mighty king who has rebelled against you, and you shall know what I will do to him and to his land; although he may have cavalry and infantry or an exceeding mighty people, I will slay them all and bring the king's head before you.

(Jasher 54:60)
Do you not know or have you not heard that our father Abraham with his servant Eliezer smote all the kings of Elam with their hosts in one night, they left not one remaining? And ever since that day our father's strength was given to us for an inheritance, for us and our seed forever.

(Jasher 54:61)
And Joseph answered and said, You speak truth, and falsehood is not in your mouth, for it was also told to us that the Hebrews have power and that the Lord their God delights much in them, and who then can stand before them?

(Jasher 54:62)
However, on this condition will I send your brother, if you will bring before me his brother the son of his mother, of whom you said that he had gone from you down to Egypt; and it shall come to pass when you bring to me his brother I will take him in his stead, because not one of you was security for him to your father, and when he shall come to me, I will then send with you his brother for whom you have been security.

(Jasher 54:63)
And Judah's anger was kindled against Joseph when he spoke this thing, and his eyes dropped blood with anger, and he said to his brothers, How does this man this day seek his own destruction and that of all Egypt!

(Jasher 54:64)
And Simeon answered Joseph, saying, Did we not tell you at first that we knew not the particular spot to which he went, and whether he be dead or alive, and why does my lord speak like to these things?

(Jasher 54:65)
And Joseph observing the countenance of Judah discerned that his anger began to kindle when he spoke to him, saying, Bring to me your other brother instead of this brother.

(Jasher 54:66)
And Joseph said to his brothers, Surely you said that your brother was either dead or lost, now if I should call him this day and he should come before you, would you give him to me instead of his brother?

(Jasher 54:67)
And Joseph began to speak and call out, Joseph, Joseph, come this day before me, and appear to your brothers and sit before them.

(Jasher 54:68)
And when Joseph spoke this thing before them, they each looked a different way to see from where Joseph would come before them.

Genesis: Chapter Forty-Five

(Genesis 45:1) (Jasher 54:69...) (Jubilees 43:14...)

And Joseph observed all their acts, and said to them, Why do you look here and there? Then Joseph saw that they were all accordant in goodness one with another, and he could not refrain himself before all them that stood by him; and he cried, Cause every man to go out from me. And there stood no man with him, while Joseph made himself known to his brothers.

(Genesis 45:2)

And he wept aloud: and the Egyptians and the house of Pharaoh heard.

(Genesis 45:3) (Jasher 54:70) (...Jubilees 43:14)

And Joseph said to his brothers, I am Joseph; does my father yet live? And his brothers were terrified at him when they heard the words of Joseph, and Judah was exceedingly terrified at him and they could not answer him; for they were troubled at his presence.

(Genesis 45:4) (...Jasher 54:69...)

And Joseph said to his brothers, Come near to me, I pray. And they came near. And he said, I am Joseph your brother, whom you sold into Egypt.

(Genesis 45:5) (...Jasher 54:69)

Now therefore do not be grieved, nor angry with yourselves,

that you sold me here: for as a support during the famine God sent me before you to preserve life.

(Genesis 45:6) (Jubilees 43:17)

For behold, these two years has the famine been in the land: and yet there are five years, in the which there shall neither be earing nor harvest or fruit of trees or ploughing.

(Genesis 45:7) (Jubilees 43:18)

And God sent me before you to set things in order that many people might live and to preserve you a posterity in the earth, and to save your lives by a great deliverance. Come down quickly you and your households, so that you perish not through the famine, and do not be grieved for your possessions.

(Genesis 45:8) (Jubilees 43:19)

So now it was not you that sent me here, but God: and tell my father that I am still alive, and you, behold, you see that the Lord has made me a father to Pharaoh, and lord of all his house, and a ruler throughout all the land of Egypt.

(Genesis 45:9)

Hurry, and go up to my father, and say to him, Thus says your son Joseph, God has made me lord of all Egypt: come down to me, do not tarry:

(Genesis 45:10)

And you shall dwell in the land of Goshen, and you shall be near to me, you, and your children, and your children's children, and your flocks, and your herds, and all that you have:

(Genesis 45:11)

And there will I nourish you; for yet there are five years of famine; lest you, and your household, and all that you have, come to poverty.

(Jubilees 43:15)

And he conversed with them in the Hebrew tongue and fell on their neck and wept.

(Genesis 45:12) (Jubilees 43:16...)

But they did not know him and they began to weep. And Joseph said, behold, your eyes see, and the eyes of my brother Benjamin, that it is my mouth that speaks to you.

(Genesis 45:13) (...Jubilees 43:16, 20)

And you shall tell my father of all my glory in Egypt, and all the riches and glory that the Lord has given me, and of all that you have seen; And he said to them: Weep not over me, but you shall hasten and bring down my father here to me.

(Genesis 45:14) (Jasher 54:71)

And when Benjamin heard the words of Joseph he was before them in the inner part of the house, and Benjamin ran to Joseph his brother, and embraced him and fell upon his neck. And Joseph fell on his brother Benjamin's neck, and wept; and Benjamin wept on his neck.

(Jasher 54:72)

And when Joseph's brothers saw that Benjamin had fallen upon his brother's neck and wept with him, they also fell upon Joseph and embraced him, and they wept a great weeping with Joseph.

(Genesis 45:15)

Moreover, Joseph kissed all his brothers, and wept on them: and after that his brothers talked with him.

(Genesis 45:16) (Jasher 54:73)

And the voice was heard in the house of Joseph that they were Joseph's brothers. And the fame thereof was heard in Pharaoh's house, saying, Joseph's brothers are come: and it pleased Pharaoh exceedingly well, and his servants, for he was afraid of them lest they should destroy Egypt.

(Jasher 54:74)

And Pharaoh sent his servants to Joseph to congratulate him concerning his brothers who had come to him, and all the captains of the armies and troops that were in Egypt came to rejoice with Joseph, and all Egypt rejoiced greatly about Joseph's brothers.

(Genesis 45:17) (Jasher 54:75...)

And Pharaoh sent his servants to Joseph, saying, Say to your brothers, Do this; lade your beasts, and go, get you to the land of Canaan;

(Genesis 45:18) (...Jasher 54:75...)

And fetch all belonging to you and take your father and your households, and come to me: and I will give you the good of the land of Egypt, and you shall eat the fat of the land.

(Genesis 45:19)

Now you are commanded, this do you; take you wagons out of the land of Egypt for your little ones, and for your wives, and bring your father, and come.

(Genesis 45:20)

Also regard not your stuff; for the good of all the land of Egypt is yours.

(Genesis 45:21) (...Jasher 54:75, 83...) (Jubilees 43:21...)

And the children of Israel did so: and Joseph gave them each fifty pieces of silver, and ten wagons, according to the commandment of the mouth of Pharaoh, and gave them provision for the way.

(Jasher 54:76)

And Joseph commanded him that was set over his house to bring out gifts and garments to his brothers, and he brought out to them many garments being robes of royalty and many gifts, and Joseph divided them among his brothers.

(Genesis 45:22) (Jasher 54:77) (...Jubilees 43:21)

To all of them he gave each man changes of many-colored raiment of gold and silver and three hundred pieces of silver; but to Benjamin he gave three hundred pieces of silver, and five changes of raiment. And Joseph commanded them all to be dressed in these garments, and to be brought before Pharaoh.

(Jasher 54:78)

And Pharaoh seeing that all Joseph's brothers were valiant men, and of beautiful appearance, he greatly rejoiced.

(Jasher 54:79)

And they afterward went out from the presence of Pharaoh to go to the land of Canaan, to their father, and their brother Benjamin was with them.

(Jasher 54:80)
And Joseph rose up and gave to them eleven chariots from Pharaoh, and Joseph gave to them his chariot, upon which he rode on the day of his being crowned in Egypt, to fetch his father to Egypt; and Joseph sent to all his brothers' children, garments according to their numbers, and a hundred pieces of silver to each of them, and he also sent garments to the wives of his brothers from the garments of the king's wives, and he sent them.

(Jasher 54:81)
And he gave to each of his brothers ten men to go with them to the land of Canaan to serve them, to serve their children and all belonging to them in coming to Egypt.

(Jasher 54:82)
And Joseph sent by the hand of his brother Benjamin ten suits of garments for his ten sons, a portion above the rest of the children of the sons of Jacob.

(Genesis 45:23) (...Jasher 54:83) (Jubilees 43:22...)
And to his father he sent after this manner; raiment and silver and ten donkeys laden with the good things of Egypt, and ten she donkeys laden with corn and bread and meat for his father and to all that were with him as provisions by the way.

(Jasher 54:84)
And he sent to his sister Dinah garments of silver and gold, and frankincense and myrrh, and aloes and women's ornaments in great plenty, and he sent the same from the wives of Pharaoh to the wives of Benjamin.

(Jasher 54:85)
And he gave to all his brothers, also to their wives, all sorts

of onyx stones and bdellium, and from all the valuable things among the great people of Egypt, nothing of all the costly things was left but what Joseph sent of to his father's household.

(Genesis 45:24...) (Jasher 54:86) (...Jubilees 43:22)
So he sent his brothers away, and they went, and he sent his brother Benjamin with them, and they departed:

(Jasher 54:87)
And Joseph went out with them to accompany them on the road to the borders of Egypt, and he commanded them concerning his father and his household, to come to Egypt.

(...Genesis 45:24) (Jasher 54:88)
And he said to them, See that you do not fall out by the way, for this thing was from the Lord to keep a great people from starvation, for there will be yet five years of famine in the land.

(Jasher 54:89)
And he commanded them, saying, When you come to the land of Canaan, do not come suddenly before my father in this affair, but act in your wisdom.

(Genesis 45:25) (Jasher 54:90)
And Joseph ceased to command them, and he turned and went back to Egypt, and the sons of Jacob went up out of Egypt, and came into the land of Canaan to Jacob their father, with joy and cheerfulness.

(Jasher 54:91)
And they came to the borders of the land, and they said to each other, What shall we do in this matter before our father, for if we come suddenly to him and tell him the matter, he will

be greatly alarmed at our words and will not believe us.

(Jasher 54:92)
And they went along until they came near their houses, and they found Serach, the daughter of Asher, going forth to meet them, and the damsel was very good and subtle, and knew how to play upon the harp.

(Jasher 54:93)
And they called to her and she came before them, and she kissed them, and they took her and gave to her a harp, saying, Go now before our father, and sit before him, and strike upon the harp, and speak these words.

(Jasher 54:94)
And they commanded her to go to their house, and she took the harp and hastened before them, and she came and sat near Jacob.

(Jasher 54:95)
And she played well and sang, and uttered in the sweetness of her words, Joseph my uncle is living, and he rules throughout the land of Egypt, and is not dead.

(Jasher 54:96)
And she continued to repeat and utter these words, and Jacob heard her words and they were agreeable to him.

(Jasher 54:97)
He listened while she repeated them twice and thrice, and joy entered the heart of Jacob at the sweetness of her words, and the spirit of God was upon him, and he knew all her words to be true.

(Jasher 54:98)
And Jacob blessed Serach when she spoke these words before him, and he said to her, My daughter, may death never prevail over you, for you have revived my spirit; only speak yet before me as you have spoken, for you have gladdened me with all your words.

(Jasher 54:99)
And she continued to sing these words, and Jacob listened and it pleased him, and he rejoiced, and the spirit of God was upon him.

(Jasher 54:100)
While he was yet speaking with her, behold his sons came to him with horses and chariots and royal garments and servants running before them.

(Jasher 54:101)
And Jacob rose up to meet them, and saw his sons dressed in royal garments and he saw all the treasures that Joseph had sent to them.

(Genesis 45:26) (Jasher 54:102, 103) (Jubilees 43:23, 24...)
And they went up and told their father, saying, Be informed that our brother Joseph is yet alive, and was measuring out corn to all the nations of the earth, and he is governor over all the land of Egypt, and it is he who spoke to us as we told you. And Jacob heard all the words of his sons, and his heart fainted, for he could not believe them for he was beside himself in his mind until he saw all that Joseph had given them and what he had sent him, and all the signs which Joseph had spoken to them.

(Genesis 45:27) (Jasher 54:104) (...Jubilees 43:24...)
And they opened out before him, and showed him all that Joseph had sent, they gave to each what Joseph had sent him, and they told him all the words of Joseph, which he had said to them. And when he saw the wagons which Joseph had sent to carry him, he knew that they had spoken the truth, and the life of the spirit of Jacob their father revived and he rejoiced exceedingly an account of his son.

(Genesis 45:28) (Jasher 54:102, 105) (...Jubilees 43:24)
And Israel said, It is enough; Joseph my son is still alive: I will go and see him before I die.

(Jasher 54:106)
And his sons told him all that had befallen them, and Jacob said, I will go down to Egypt to see my son and his offspring.

(Jasher 54:107)
And Jacob rose up and put on the garments which Joseph had sent him, and after he had washed, and shaved his hair, he put upon his head the turban which Joseph had sent him.

(Jasher 54:108)
And all the people of Jacob's house and their wives put on the garments which Joseph had sent to them, and they greatly rejoiced at Joseph that he was still living and that he was ruling in Egypt,

(Jasher 54:109)
And all the inhabitants of Canaan heard of this thing, and they came and rejoiced much with Jacob that he was still living.

(Jasher 54:110)
And Jacob made a feast for them for three days, and all the

kings of Canaan and nobles of the land ate and drank and rejoiced in the house of Jacob.

Genesis: Chapter Forty-Six

(Jasher 55:1)
And it came to pass after this that Jacob said, I will go and see my son in Egypt and will then come back to the land of Canaan of which God had spoken to Abraham, for I cannot leave the land of my birthplace.

(Genesis 46:1) (Jubilees 44:1)
And Israel took his journey with all that he had, from Haran from his house on the new moon of the third month, and he went on the way of the Well of the Oath, and came to Beersheba, and offered sacrifices to the God of his father Isaac on the seventh of this month.

(Jubilees 44:2)
And Jacob remembered the dream that he had seen at Bethel, and he feared to go down into Egypt.

(Jubilees 44:3)
And while he was thinking of sending word to Joseph to come to him, and that he would not go down, he remained there seven days, if perchance he could see a vision as to whether he should remain or go down.

(Jubilees 44:4)
And he celebrated the harvest festival of the first-fruits with old grain, for in all the land of Canaan there was not a handful of seed in the land, for the famine was over all the beasts and cattle and birds, and also over man.

(Genesis 46:2) (Jasher 55:2...) (Jubilees 44:5...)

And on the sixteenth the Lord appeared to him, and God spoke to Israel in the visions of the night, and said, Jacob, Jacob. And he said, Here am I.

(Genesis 46:3) (...Jasher 55:2) (...Jubilees 44:5..., 6)

And he said to him, I am God, the God of your fathers, the God of Abraham and Isaac. Fear not; Go down to Egypt with all your household and remain there; fear not to go down into Egypt; for I will there make of you a great nation:

(Genesis 46:4) (...Jubilees 44:5)

I will go down with you into Egypt; and I will also surely bring you up again, and in this land, you shall be buried, and Joseph shall put his hand on your eyes.

(Jasher 55:3)

And Jacob said within himself, I will go and see my son whether the fear of his God is yet in his heart amidst all the inhabitants of Egypt.

(Jasher 55:4)

And the Lord said to Jacob, Do not fear about Joseph, for he still retains his integrity to serve me, as will seem good in your sight, and Jacob rejoiced exceedingly concerning his son.

(Genesis 46:5) (Jasher 55:5) (Jubilees 44:7)

At that time Jacob commanded his sons and household to go to Egypt according to the word of the Lord to him, and Jacob rose up with his sons, and his sons' sons, and all his household, and he went out from the land of Canaan from Beersheba with joy and gladness of heart, and they went to the land of Egypt. And the sons of Israel carried Jacob their father, and their little ones, and their wives, and their possessions in the wagons which Pharaoh had sent to carry him.

(Jubilees 44:8)
And Israel rose up from the Well of the Oath on the sixteenth of this third month, and he went to the land of Egypt.

(Genesis 46:6)
And they took their cattle, and their goods, which they had gotten in the land of Canaan, and came into Egypt, Jacob, and all his seed with him:

(Genesis 46:7)
His sons, and his sons' sons with him, his daughters, and his sons' daughters, and all his seed brought he with him into Egypt.

(Genesis 46:8) (Jasher 59:1, 6) (Jubilees 44:11, 12...)
And these are the names of the children of Israel, who dwelt in Egypt, which came into Egypt with Jacob their father; all the sons of Jacob came to Egypt, every man with his household. And these were their offspring that were born to them in the land of Canaan, before they came to Egypt with their father Jacob. Jacob and his sons: Reuben, Jacob's firstborn.

(Genesis 46:9) (Jasher 59:7) (...Jubilees 44:12)
And these are the names of the sons of Reuben; Hanoch, and Phallu, and Hezron, and Carmi - five.

(Genesis 46:10) (Jasher 59:8) (Jubilees 44:13)
Simeon and his sons; and these are the names of the sons of Simeon; Jemuel, and Jamin, and Ohad, and Jachin, and Zohar, and Shaul the son of a Canaanitish woman - seven.

(Genesis 46:11) (Jasher 59:9) (Jubilees 44:14)

Levi and his sons; and these are the names of the sons of Levi; Gershon, Kohath, and Merari – four - and their sister Jochebed, who was born to them in their going down to Egypt.

(Genesis 46:12) (Jasher 59:10, 11) (Jubilees 44:15)

Judah and his sons; and these are the names of the sons of Judah; Er, and Onan, and Shelah, and Pharez, and Zerah: but Er and Onan died in the land of Canaan - four. And the sons of Pharez were Hezron and Hamul.

(Genesis 46:13) (Jasher 59:12) (Jubilees 44:16)

Issachar and his sons; and these are the names of the sons of Issachar; Tola, and Phuvah, and Job, and Shimron - five.

(Genesis 46:14) (Jasher 59:13...) (Jubilees 44:17)

Zebulon and his sons; and these are the names of the sons of Zebulun; Sered, and Elon, and Jahleel - four.

(Genesis 46:15) (Jasher 59:2) (Jubilees 44:18)

These are the sons of Jacob and their sons whom Leah, which she bore to Jacob in Padanaram in Mesopotamia, Reuben, Simeon, Levi, Judah, Issachar and Zebulun - six, and their one sister, his daughter Dinah: all the souls of his sons of Leah, and their sons, who went with Jacob their father into Egypt, were twenty-nine, and Jacob their father being with them, they were thirty, and his daughters were thirty and three.

(Jasher 59:4) (Jubilees 44:19)

And the sons of Zilpah, Leah's handmaid, the wife of Jacob, who bore to Jacob were Gad and Ashur.

(Genesis 46:16) (Jasher 59:15) (Jubilees 44:20)

And these are the names of their sons who went with him

into Egypt. The sons of Gad; Ziphion, and Haggi, Shuni, and Ezbon, Eri, and Arodi, and Areli - eight.

(Genesis 46:17) (Jasher 59:16) (Jubilees 44:21)
And the sons of Asher; Jimnah, and Ishuah, and Isui, and Beriah, and Serah their one sister - six: and the sons of Beriah; Heber, and Malchiel.

(Genesis 46:18) (Jubilees 44:22)
These are the sons of Zilpah, whom Laban gave to Leah his daughter, and these she bore to Jacob, even sixteen souls, and all those of Leah were forty-four.

(Genesis 46:19) (Jasher 59:3) (Jubilees 44:23)
And the sons of Rachel, Jacob's wife, were Joseph, and Benjamin.

(Genesis 46:20) (Jasher 59:18) (Jubilees 44:24)
And to Joseph in the land of Egypt were born before his father came into Egypt, Manasseh and Ephraim, those which Asenath the daughter of Potipherah priest of On bore to him - three.

(Genesis 46:21) (Jasher 59:17) (Jubilees 44:25)
And the sons of Benjamin were Belah, and Becher, and Ashbel, Gera, and Naaman, Ehi, and Rosh, Muppim, and Huppim, and Ard - eleven.

(Genesis 46:22) (Jubilees 44:26)
These are the sons of Rachel, which were born to Jacob: all the souls were fourteen.

(Jasher 59:5) (Jubilees 44:27)
And the sons of Bilhah, the handmaid of Rachel, the wife of

Jacob, whom she bore to Jacob, were Dan and Naphtali.

(Genesis 46:23) (...Jasher 59:13) (Jubilees 44:28)
And these are the names of their sons who went with them into Egypt. And the sons of Dan; Hushim and Samon, and Asudi. And 'Ijaka, and Salomon - six.

(Jubilees 44:29)
And they died the year in which they entered into Egypt, and there was left to Dan Hushim alone.

(Genesis 46:24) (Jasher 59:14) (Jubilees 44:30)
And these are the names of the sons of Naphtali; Jahzeel, and Guni, and Jezer, and Shillem, and Iv.

(Jubilees 44:31)
And Iv, who was born after the years of famine, died in Egypt.

(Genesis 46:25) (Jubilees 44:32)
These are the sons of Bilhah, which Laban gave to Rachel his daughter, and she bore these to Jacob: all the souls were seven. And all the souls of Rachel were twenty-six.

(Genesis 46:26) (Jasher 59:19...)
And all the souls that came with Jacob into Egypt to dwell there, which came out of his loins, besides Jacob's sons' wives, all the souls were sixty-six;

(Genesis 46:27) (...Jasher 59:19...) (Jubilees 44:33)
And the sons of Joseph, which were born him in Egypt, were two souls: all the souls of the house of Jacob, which came into Egypt, were seventy. These are his children and his children's children, in all seventy, but five died in Egypt before Joseph,

and had no children.

(Jubilees 44:34)
And in the land of Canaan two sons of Judah died, Er and Onan, and they had no children, and the children of Israel buried those who perished, and they were reckoned among the seventy Gentile nations.

(Genesis 46:28...) (Jasher 55:6...) (Jubilees 44:9)
And it came to pass when they came near Egypt, Jacob sent Judah before him to his son Joseph, that he might show him a situation in Egypt, to examine the Land of Goshen, and to direct his face to Goshen, for Joseph had told his brothers that they should come and dwell there that they might be near him.

(Jubilees 44:10)
And this was the goodliest in the land of Egypt, and near to him, for all of them and also for the cattle.

(...Jasher 55:6)
And Judah did according to the word of his father, and he hastened and ran and came to Joseph, and they assigned for them a place in the land of Goshen for all his household and Judah returned and came along the road to his father.

(...Genesis 46:28) (Jubilees 45:1)
And Israel went into the country of Egypt, and they came into the land of Goshen, on the new moon of the fourth month, in the second year of the third week of the forty-fifth jubilee.

(Genesis 46:29...) (Jasher 55:7, 8, 9)
And Joseph made ready his chariot, and he assembled all his mighty men and his servants and all the officers of Egypt in

order to go and meet his father Jacob, and Joseph's mandate was proclaimed in Egypt, saying, All that do not go to meet Jacob shall die.

(...Genesis 46:29...) (Jasher 55:8) (Jubilees 45:2...)
And on the next day Joseph went up with all Egypt a great and mighty host, all dressed in garments of fine linen and purple and with instruments of silver and gold and with their instruments of war with them.

(...Genesis 46:29...) (Jasher 55:9) (...Jubilees 45:2...)
And they all went to meet Israel his father, to the land of Goshen, with all sorts of musical instruments, with drums and timbrels, strewing myrrh and aloes all along the road, and they all went after this fashion, and the earth shook at their shouting.

(Jasher 55:10)
And all the women of Egypt went upon the roofs of Egypt and upon the walls to meet Jacob, and upon the head of Joseph was Pharaoh's regal crown, for Pharaoh had sent it to him to put on at the time of his going to meet his father.

(Jasher 55:11)
And when Joseph came within fifty cubits of his father, he alighted from the chariot and he walked toward his father, and when all the officers of Egypt and her nobles saw that Joseph had gone on foot toward his father, they also alighted and walked on foot toward Jacob.

(Jasher 55:12)
And when Jacob approached the camp of Joseph, Jacob observed the camp that was coming toward him with Joseph, and it gratified him and Jacob was astonished at it.

(Jasher 55:13)
And Jacob said to Judah, Who is that man whom I see in the camp of Egypt dressed in kingly robes with a very red garment upon him and a royal crown upon his head, who has alighted from his chariot and is coming toward us? And Judah answered his father, saying, He is your son Joseph the king; and Jacob rejoiced in seeing the glory of his son.

(...Genesis 46:29) (Jasher 55:14, 15) (...Jubilees 45:2)
And Joseph came near his father and he bowed to his father, and presented himself to him; and all the men of the camp bowed to the ground with him before Jacob. And behold Jacob ran and hastened to his son Joseph and fell on his neck, and kissed him, and they wept, and Joseph also embraced his father and he fell on his father's neck and kissed him, and wept on his neck a good while; and they wept and all the people of Egypt wept with them.

(Genesis 46:30) (Jasher 55:16) (Jubilees 45:3)
And Israel said to Joseph, Now let me die cheerfully, since I have seen your face, because you are yet alive and with glory. And now may the Lord God of Israel be blessed the God of Abraham and the God of Isaac who has not withheld His mercy and His grace from His servant Jacob.

(Jubilees 45:4)
It is enough for me that I have seen your face whilst I am yet alive; yea, true is the vision which I saw at Bethel. Blessed be the Lord my God forever and ever, and blessed be His name.

(Jasher 55:17)
And the sons of Jacob and their wives and their children and their servants, and all the household of Jacob wept exceedingly with Joseph, and they kissed him and wept greatly with him.

(Jubilees 45:5)
And Joseph and his brothers ate bread before their father and drank wine, and Jacob rejoiced with exceeding great joy because he saw Joseph eating with his brothers and drinking before him, and he blessed the Creator of all things who had preserved him, and had preserved for him his twelve sons.

(Jasher 55:18...)
And Joseph and all his people returned afterward home to Egypt, and Jacob and his sons and all the children of his household came with Joseph to Egypt.

(Genesis 46:31) (Jasher 55:19)
And Joseph said to his father and to his brothers, and to his father's house, I will go up, and show Pharaoh, and say to him, My brothers, and my father's house and all belonging to them, which were in the land of Canaan, are come to me; and behold they are in the land of Goshen.

(Genesis 46:32)
And the men are shepherds, for their trade has been to feed cattle; and they have brought their flocks, and their herds, and all that they have.

(Genesis 46:33)
And it shall come to pass, when Pharaoh shall call you, and shall say, What is your occupation?

(Genesis 46:34)
That you shall say, Your servants' trade has been about cattle from our youth even until now, both we, and also our fathers: that you may dwell in the land of Goshen; for every shepherd is an abomination to the Egyptians.

Genesis: Chapter Forty-Seven

(Genesis 47:1) (Jasher 55:20...)

Then Joseph came and told Pharaoh, and said, My father and my brothers, and their flocks, and their herds, and all that they have, are come out of the land of Canaan; and, behold, they are in the land of Goshen.

(Genesis 47:2) (...Jasher 55:20)

And he took some of his brothers, Reuben, Issachar Zebulun and his brother Benjamin, even five men, and presented them to Pharaoh.

(Jasher 55:21)

And Joseph spoke to Pharaoh, saying, My brothers and my father's household and all belonging to them, together with their flocks and cattle have come to me from the land of Canaan, to sojourn in Egypt; for the famine was sore upon them.

(Genesis 47:3)

And Pharaoh said to his brothers, What is your occupation? And they said to Pharaoh, Your servants are shepherds, both we, and also our fathers.

(Genesis 47:4)

They said moreover to Pharaoh, For to sojourn in the land are we come; for your servants have no pasture for their flocks; for the famine is sore in the land of Canaan: now therefore, we pray, let your servants dwell in the land of Goshen.

(Genesis 47:5)

And Pharaoh spoke to Joseph, saying, Your father and your brothers are come to you:

(Genesis 47:6...) (Jasher 55:22)

And Pharaoh said to Joseph, The land of Egypt is before you; in the best of the land make your father and brothers to dwell; withhold not from them all that is good, and cause them to eat of the fat of the land.

(Jasher 55:23)

And Joseph answered, saying, Behold I have stationed them in the land of Goshen, for they are shepherds, therefore let them remain in Goshen to feed their flocks apart from the Egyptians.

(...Genesis 47:6) (Jasher 55:24...)

And Pharaoh said to Joseph, Do with your brothers all that they shall say to you; in the land of Goshen let them dwell: And if you know any men of activity among them, then make them rulers over my cattle. And the sons of Jacob bowed down to Pharaoh, and they went forth from him in peace.

(Genesis 47:7) (...Jasher 55:24, 25...)

And afterward Joseph brought in Jacob his father, and set him before Pharaoh: And Jacob came and bowed down to Pharaoh, and Jacob blessed Pharaoh.

(Genesis 47:8)

And Pharaoh said to Jacob, How old are you?

(Genesis 47:9)

And Jacob said to Pharaoh, The days of the years of my pilgrimage are a hundred and thirty years: few and evil have the days of the years of my life been, and have not attained to the days of the years of the life of my fathers in the days of their pilgrimage.

(Genesis 47:10) (...Jasher 55:25...)
And Jacob blessed Pharaoh, and went out from before Pharaoh.

(Jubilees 45:6...)
And Joseph had given to his father and to his brothers as a gift the right of dwelling in the land of Goshen and in Rameses and all the region round about, which he ruled over before Pharaoh.

(Genesis 47:11) (...Jasher 55:18, ...25) (...Jubilees 45:6)
And Joseph placed his father and his brothers, and gave them a possession in the land of Egypt, in the best of Egypt, in the land of Goshen, in the land of Rameses, as Pharaoh had commanded; and Jacob and all his sons, and all his household dwelt in the land of Goshen. And Israel was one hundred and thirty years old when he came into Egypt.

(Genesis 47:12) (Jasher 55:26) (Jubilees 45:7)
And in the second year, that is in the hundred and thirtieth year of the life of Jacob, Joseph nourished his father, and his brothers, and all his father's household, and also their possessions with bread, according to their families, all the days of the famine; they lacked nothing - as much as sufficed them for the seven years of the famine.

(Jasher 55:27)
And Joseph gave to them the best part of the whole land; the best of Egypt had they all the days of Joseph; and Joseph also gave to them and to the whole of his father's household,

clothes and garments year by year; and the sons of Jacob remained securely in Egypt all the days of their brother.

(Jasher 55:28)
And Jacob always ate at Joseph's table, Jacob and his sons did not leave Joseph's table day or night, besides what Jacob's children consumed in their houses.

(Genesis 47:13) (Jubilees 45:8...)

And there was no bread in all the land; for the famine was very sore, so that the land of Egypt and all the land of Canaan fainted by reason of the famine.

(Genesis 47:14)

And Joseph gathered up all the money that was found in the land of Egypt, and in the land of Canaan, for the corn which they bought: and Joseph brought the money into Pharaoh's house.

(Genesis 47:15)

And when money failed in the land of Egypt, and in the land of Canaan, all the Egyptians came to Joseph, and said, Give us bread: for why should we die in your presence? For the money fails.

(Genesis 47:16)

And Joseph said, Give your cattle; and I will give you for your cattle, if money fail.

(Genesis 47:17)

And they brought their cattle to Joseph: and Joseph gave them bread in exchange for horses, and for the flocks, and for the cattle of the herds, and for the donkeys: and he fed them with bread for all their cattle for that year.

(Jasher 55:29)
And all Egypt ate bread during the days of the famine from the house of Joseph, for all the Egyptians sold all belonging to them on account of the famine.

(Genesis 47:18)
When that year was ended, they came to him the second year, and said to him, We will not hide it from my lord, how that our money is spent; my lord also has our herds of cattle; there is not ought left in the sight of my lord, but our bodies, and our lands:

(Genesis 47:19)
Why shall we die before your eyes, both we and our land? Buy us and our land for bread, and we and our land will be servants to Pharaoh: and give us seed, that we may live, and not die, that the land be not desolate.

(Genesis 47:20) (Jasher 55:30) (...Jubilees 45:8...)
And Joseph bought all the lands and fields of Egypt for bread on the account of Pharaoh; for the Egyptians sold every man his field, because the famine prevailed over them: so the land became Pharaoh's. And Joseph supplied all Egypt with bread all the days of the famine, and Joseph collected all the silver and gold that came to him for the corn which they bought throughout the land, and he accumulated much gold and silver, besides an immense quantity of onyx stones, bdellium and valuable garments which they brought to Joseph from every part of the land when their money was spent.

(Jasher 55:31)
And Joseph took all the silver and gold that came into his hand, about seventy-two talents of gold and silver, and also onyx stones and bdellium in great abundance, and Joseph went and concealed them in four parts, and he concealed one

part in the wilderness near the Red sea, and one part by the river Perath, and the third and fourth part he concealed in the desert opposite to the wilderness of Persia and Media.

(Jasher 55:32)
And he took part of the gold and silver that was left, and gave it to all his brothers and to all his father's household, and to all the women of his father's household, and the rest he brought to the house of Pharaoh, about twenty talents of gold and silver.

(Jasher 55:33...)
And Joseph gave all the gold and silver that was left to Pharaoh, and Pharaoh placed it in the treasury.

(Genesis 47:21)
And as for the people, he removed them to cities from one end of the borders of Egypt even to the other end thereof.

(Genesis 47:22)
Only the land of the priests bought he not; for the priests had a portion assigned them of Pharaoh, and ate their portion which Pharaoh gave them: why they sold not their lands.

(Genesis 47:23)
Then Joseph said to the people, Behold, I have bought you this day and your land for Pharaoh: lo, here is seed for you, and you shall sow the land.

(Genesis 47:24)
And it shall come to pass in the increase, that you shall give the fifth pare to Pharaoh, and four pares shall be your own, for seed of the field, and for your food, and for them of your

households, and for food for your little ones.

(Genesis 47:25)

And they said, You have saved our lives: let us find grace in the sight of my lord, and we will be Pharaoh's servants.

(...Jubilees 45:8)

Thus Joseph got possession of the people and their cattle and everything for Pharaoh.

(...Jasher 55:33...) (Jubilees 45:9)

And the days of the famine ceased after that in the land. And Joseph gave to the people in the land seed and food that they might sow in the eighth year, for the river had overflowed all the land of Egypt.

(...Jasher 55:33) (Jubilees 45:10)

For in the seven years of the famine it had (not) overflowed and had irrigated only a few places on the banks of the river, but now it overflowed and the Egyptians sowed and reaped in the whole land, and it bore much corn that year, and they obtained their usual quantity year by year; they lacked nothing.

(Jubilees 45:11)

And this was the first year of the fourth week of the forty-fifth jubilee.

(Genesis 47:26) (Jubilees 45:12)

And Joseph took of the corn of the harvest the fifth part for the king and left four parts for them for food and for seed, and Joseph made it a law over the land of Egypt to this day, that Pharaoh should have the fifth pare; except the land of the priests only, which became not Pharaoh's.

(Jasher 55:34...)
And Joseph dwelt securely in Egypt, and the whole land was under his advice.

(Jasher 55:35)
And Joseph was very aged, advanced in days, and his two sons, Ephraim and Manasseh, remained constantly in the house of Jacob, together with the children of the sons of Jacob their brothers, to learn the ways of the Lord and his law.

(Genesis 47:27) (...Jasher 55:34, 36)
And Israel and his sons, his father and all his brothers dwelt in the land of Egypt, in the country of Goshen and took possession of it; and they had possessions therein, and grew, and multiplied exceedingly in it.

(Genesis 47:28) (Jasher 56:1) (Jubilees 45:13...)
And Jacob lived in the land of Egypt seventeen years: and all the days which he lived were three jubilees, so the whole age of Jacob was a hundred forty seven years.

(Genesis 47:29...) (Jasher 56:2)
At that time Jacob was attacked with that illness of which he died. And the time drew near that Israel must die: and he sent and called his son Joseph from Egypt, and Joseph his son came from Egypt and Joseph came to his father.

(...Genesis 47:29) (Jasher 56:3...)
And Jacob said to him and to his sons, Behold I die, and the God of your ancestors will visit you, and bring you back to the land, which the Lord swore to give to you and to your children after you, If now I have found grace in your sight, put, I pray, your hand under my thigh, and deal kindly and truly with me;

now therefore when I am dead, do not bury me, I pray, in Egypt:

(Genesis 47:30) (...Jasher 56:3)

But bury me in the cave which is in Machpelah in Hebron in the land of Canaan, near my ancestors. I will lie with my fathers, and you shall carry me out of Egypt, and bury me in their burying place. And he said, I will do as you have said.

(Genesis 47:31...) (Jasher 56:4)

And Jacob made his sons swear to bury him in Machpelah, in Hebron, And he said, Swear to me. And he and his sons swore to him concerning this thing.

(Jasher 56:5)

And he commanded them, saying, Serve the Lord your God, for he who delivered your fathers will also deliver you from all trouble.

(Jasher 56:6)

And Jacob said, Call all your children to me, and all the children of Jacob's sons came and sat before him, and Jacob blessed them, and he said to them, The Lord God of your fathers shall grant you a thousand times as much and bless you, and may he give you the blessing of your father Abraham; and all the children of Jacob's sons went forth on that day after he had blessed them.

(...Genesis 47:31)

And Israel bowed himself on the bed's head.

Genesis: Chapter Forty-Eight

(Genesis 48:1)
And it came to pass after these things, that one told Joseph, Behold, your father is sick: and he took with him his two sons, Manasseh and Ephraim.

(Genesis 48:2)
And one told Jacob, and said, Behold, your son Joseph comes to you: and Israel strengthened himself, and sat on the bed.

(Genesis 48:3)
And Jacob said to Joseph, God Almighty appeared to me at Luz in the land of Canaan, and blessed me,

(Genesis 48:4)
And said to me, Behold, I will make you fruitful, and multiply you, and I will make of you a multitude of people; and will give this land to your seed after you for an everlasting possession.

(Genesis 48:5)
And now your two sons, Ephraim and Manasseh, which were born to you in the land of Egypt before I came to you into Egypt, are mine; as Reuben and Simeon, they shall be mine.

(Genesis 48:6)
And your kids, which you have after them, shall be yours, and shall be called after the name of their brothers in their inheritance.

(Genesis 48:7)

And as for me, when I came from Padan, Rachel died by me in the land of Canaan in the way, when yet there was but a little way to come to Ephrath: and I buried her there in the way of Ephrath; the same is Bethlehem.

(Genesis 48:8)

And Israel beheld Joseph's sons, and said, Who are these?

(Genesis 48:9)

And Joseph said to his father, They are my sons, whom God has given me in this place. And he said, Bring them, I pray, to me, and I will bless them.

(Genesis 48:10)

Now the eyes of Israel were dim for age, so that he could not see. And he brought them near to him; and he kissed them, and embraced them.

(Genesis 48:11)

And Israel said to Joseph, I had not thought to see your face: and, lo, God has showed me also your seed.

(Genesis 48:12)

And Joseph brought them out from between his knees, and he bowed himself with his face to the earth.

(Genesis 48:13)

And Joseph took them both, Ephraim in his right hand toward Israel's left hand, and Manasseh in his left hand toward Israel's right hand, and brought them near to him.

(Genesis 48:14)

And Israel stretched out his right hand, and laid it on

Ephraim's head, who was the younger, and his left hand on Manasseh's head, guiding his hands wittingly; for Manasseh was the firstborn.

(Genesis 48:15)

And he blessed Joseph, and said, God, before whom my fathers Abraham and Isaac walked, the God which fed me all my life long to this day,

(Genesis 48:16)

The Angel which redeemed me from all evil, bless the lads; and let my name be named on them, and the name of my fathers Abraham and Isaac; and let them grow into a multitude in the midst of the earth.

(Genesis 48:17)

And when Joseph saw that his father laid his right hand on the head of Ephraim, it displeased him: and he held up his father's hand, to remove it from Ephraim's head to Manasseh's head.

(Genesis 48:18)

And Joseph said to his father, Not so, my father: for this is the firstborn; put your right hand on his head.

(Genesis 48:19)

And his father refused, and said, I know it, my son, I know it: he also shall become a people, and he also shall be great: but truly his younger brother shall be greater than he, and his seed shall become a multitude of nations.

(Genesis 48:20)

And he blessed them that day, saying, In you shall Israel bless, saying, God make you as Ephraim and as Manasseh: and he set Ephraim before Manasseh.

(Genesis 48:21)

And Israel said to Joseph, Behold, I die: but God shall be with you, and bring you again to the land of your fathers.

(Genesis 48:22)

Moreover, I have given to you one portion above your brothers, which I took out of the hand of the Amorite with my sword and with my bow.

Genesis: Chapter Forty-Nine

(Genesis 49:1) (Jasher 56:7)

And on the next day Jacob again called to his sons, and they all assembled and came to him and sat before him, and Jacob on that day blessed his sons before his death, each man he blessed according to his blessing; behold it is written in the book of the law of the Lord appertaining to Israel. And Jacob said, Gather yourselves together, that I may tell you that which shall befall you in the last days.

(Genesis 49:2)

Gather yourselves together, and hear, you sons of Jacob; and hearken to Israel your father.

(Genesis 49:3)

Reuben, you are my firstborn, my might, and the beginning of my strength, the excellency of dignity, and the excellency of power:

(Genesis 49:4)

Unstable as water, you shall not excel; because you went up to your father's bed; then you defiled it: he went up to my couch.

(Genesis 49:5)

Simeon and Levi are brothers; instruments of cruelty are in their habitations.

(Genesis 49:6)

O my soul, come not you into their secret; to their assembly, my honor, be not you united: for in their anger they slew a man, and in their self-will they dug down a wall.

(Genesis 49:7)

Cursed be their anger, for it was fierce; and their wrath, for it was cruel: I will divide them in Jacob, and scatter them in Israel.

(Genesis 49:8) (Jasher 56:8)

And Jacob said to Judah: Judah, I know my son that you are a mighty man for your brothers; you are he whom your brothers shall praise: your hand shall be in the neck of your enemies; your father's children shall bow down before you, reign over them, and your sons shall reign over their sons forever.

(Jasher 56:9)

Only teach your sons the bow and all the weapons of war, in order that they may fight the battles of their brother who will rule over his enemies.

(Genesis 49:9)

Judah is a lion's whelp: from the prey, my son, you are gone up: he stooped down, he couched as a lion, and as an old lion; who shall rouse him up?

(Genesis 49:10)

The scepter shall not depart from Judah, nor a lawgiver from between his feet, until Shiloh come; and to him shall the gathering of the people be.

(Genesis 49:11)

Binding his foal to the vine, and his donkey's colt to the choice vine; he washed his garments in wine, and his clothes in the blood of grapes:

(Genesis 49:12)
His eyes shall be red with wine, and his teeth white with milk.

(Genesis 49:13)
Zebulun shall dwell at the haven of the sea; and he shall be for a haven of ships; and his border shall be to Zidon.

(Genesis 49:14)
Issachar is a strong donkey couching down between two burdens:

(Genesis 49:15)
And he saw that rest was good, and the land that it was pleasant; and bowed his shoulder to bear, and became a servant to tribute.

(Genesis 49:16)
Dan shall judge his people, as one of the tribes of Israel.

(Genesis 49:17)
Dan shall be a serpent by the way, an adder in the path, that bites the horse heels, so that his rider shall fall backward.

(Genesis 49:18)
I have waited for your salvation, O LORD.

(Genesis 49:19)
Gad, a troop shall overcome him: but he shall overcome at the last.

(Genesis 49:20)
Out of Asher his bread shall be fat, and he shall yield royal dainties.

(Genesis 49:21)

Naphtali is a hind let loose: he giveth goodly words.

(Genesis 49:22)

Joseph is a fruitful bough, even a fruitful bough by a well; whose branches run over the wall:

(Genesis 49:23)

The archers have sorely grieved him, and shot at him, and hated him:

(Genesis 49:24)

But his bow abode in strength, and the arms of his hands were made strong by the hands of the mighty God of Jacob; (from there is the shepherd, the stone of Israel:)

(Genesis 49:25)

Even by the God of your father, who shall help you; and by the Almighty, who shall bless you with blessings of heaven above, blessings of the deep that lie under, blessings of the breasts, and of the womb:

(Genesis 49:26)

The blessings of your father have prevailed above the blessings of my progenitors to the utmost bound of the everlasting hills: they shall be on the head of Joseph, and on the crown of the head of him that was separate from his brothers.

(Genesis 49:27)

Benjamin shall ravin as a wolf: in the morning, he shall devour the prey, and at night he shall divide the spoil.

(Genesis 49:28)

All these are the twelve tribes of Israel: and this is it that their father spoke to them, and blessed them; everyone according to his blessing he blessed them.

(Genesis 49:29) (Jasher 56:10...)

And Jacob again charged his sons on that day, and said to them, I am to be gathered this day to my people: carry me up from Egypt, and bury me with my fathers in the cave that is in the field of Ephron the Hittite, as I have commanded you.

(Genesis 49:30) (...Jasher 56:10)

In the cave that is in the field of Machpelah, which is before Mamre, in the land of Canaan, which Abraham bought with the field of Ephron the Hittite for a possession of a burying place,

(Genesis 49:31)

There they buried Abraham and Sarah his wife; there they buried Isaac and Rebekah his wife; and there I buried Leah.

(Genesis 49:32)

The purchase of the field and of the cave that is therein was from the children of Heth.

(Jasher 56:11)
Howbeit take heed I pray you that none of your sons carry me, only yourselves, and this is the manner you shall do to me, when you carry my body to go with it to the land of Canaan to bury me,

(Jasher 56:12)
Judah, Issachar and Zebulun shall carry my bier at the eastern side; Reuben, Simeon and Gad at the south, Ephraim, Manasseh and Benjamin at the west, Dan, Asher and Naphtali at the north.

(Jasher 56:13)
Let not Levi carry with you, for he and his sons will carry the ark of the covenant of the Lord with the Israelites in the camp, neither let Joseph my son carry, for as a king so let his glory be; howbeit, Ephraim and Manasseh shall be in their stead.

(Jasher 56:14)
Thus you shall do to me when you carry me away; do not neglect any thing of all that I command you; and it shall come to pass when you do this to me, that the Lord will remember you favorably and your children after you forever.

(Jasher 56:15)
And you my sons, honor each his brother and his relative, and command your children and your children's children after you to serve the Lord God of your ancestors all the days.

(Jasher 56:16)
In order that you may prolong your days in the land, you and your children and your children's children forever, when you do what is good and upright in the sight of the Lord your God, to go in all his ways.

(Jasher 56:17)
And you, Joseph my son, forgive I pray you the prongs of your brothers and all their misdeeds in the injury that they heaped upon you, for God intended it for your and your children's benefit.

(Jasher 56:18)
And O my son, do not leave your brothers to the inhabitants of Egypt, neither hurt their feelings, for behold I consign them to the hand of God and in your hand to guard them from the Egyptians; and the sons of Jacob answered their father

saying, O, our father, all that you have commanded us, so will we do; may God only be with us.

(Jasher 56:19)
And Jacob said to his sons, So may God be with you when you keep all his ways; turn not from his ways either to the right or the left in performing what is good and upright in his sight.

(Jasher 56:20)
For I know that many and grievous troubles will befall you in the latter days in the land, yea your children and children's children, only serve the Lord and he will save you from all trouble.

(Jasher 56:21)
And it shall come to pass when you shall go after God to serve him and will teach your children after you, and your children's children, to know the Lord, then will the Lord raise up to you and your children a servant from among your children, and the Lord will deliver you through his hand from all affliction, and bring you out of Egypt and bring you back to the land of your fathers to inherit it securely.

(Genesis 49:33) (Jasher 56:22)

And when Jacob had made an end of commanding his sons, he gathered up his feet into the bed, and yielded up the ghost, and was gathered to his people.

(...Jubilees 45:13)
And Israel died in the fourth year of the fifth week of the forty-fifth jubilee.

(Jubilees 45:14)
And Israel blessed his sons before he died and told them

everything that would befall them in the land of Egypt; and he made known to them what would come on them in the last days, and blessed them and gave to Joseph two portions in the land.

Genesis: Chapter Fifty

(Genesis 50:1) (Jasher 56:23)

And Joseph fell on his father's face, and he cried out and wept on him, and kissed him, and he called out in a bitter voice, and he said, O my father, my father.

(Jasher 56:24)

And his son's wives and all his household came and fell upon Jacob, and they wept over him, and cried in a very loud voice concerning Jacob.

(Jasher 56:25)

And all the sons of Jacob rose up together, and they tore their garments, and they all put sackcloth upon their loins, and they fell upon their faces, and they cast dust upon their heads toward the heavens.

(Jasher 56:26)

And the thing was told to Osnath Joseph's wife, and she rose up and put on a sack and she with all the Egyptian women with her came and mourned and wept for Jacob.

(Jasher 56:27)

And also all the people of Egypt who knew Jacob came all on that day when they heard this thing, and all Egypt wept for many days.

(Genesis 50:2) (Jasher 56:29)

And it came to pass after this that Joseph commanded his servants the physicians to embalm his father with myrrh and frankincense and all manner of incense and perfume: and the physicians embalmed Israel as Joseph had commanded them.

(Genesis 50:3) (Jasher 56:28, 30)
And forty days were fulfilled for him; for so are fulfilled the days of those which are embalmed: and all the Egyptians and the elders and all the inhabitants of the land of Goshen wept and mourned over Jacob, and all his sons and the children of his household lamented and mourned over their father Jacob many days. And also, the women from the land of Canaan came to Egypt when they heard that Jacob was dead, and they wept for him in Egypt for seventy days.

(Genesis 50:4) (Jasher 56:31...)
And when the days of his mourning were passed away, at the end of seventy days, Joseph spoke to the house of Pharaoh, saying, If now I have found grace in your eyes, speak, I pray, in the ears of Pharaoh, saying,

(Genesis 50:5) (...Jasher 56:31)
My father made me swear, saying, Lo, I die: in my grave which I dug for me in the land of Canaan, there shall you bury me. Now therefore let me go up, I pray, and bury my father, and I will come again.

(Genesis 50:6) (Jasher 56:32...)
And Pharaoh sent Joseph saying, Go up, and bury your father, according as he said, and as he made you swear.

(Genesis 50:7...) (...Jasher 56:32)
And Joseph went up with all his brothers to go to the land of Canaan to bury his father Jacob as he had commanded them.

(Jasher 56:33)
And Pharaoh commanded that it should be proclaimed throughout Egypt, saying, Whoever does not go up with Joseph and his brothers to the land of Canaan to bury Jacob, shall die.

(...Genesis 50:7) (Jasher 56:34)

And all Egypt heard of Pharaoh's proclamation, and they all rose up together, and all the servants of Pharaoh, the elders of his house, and all the elders of the land of Egypt went up with Joseph, and all the officers and nobles of Pharaoh went up as the servants of Joseph, and they went to bury Jacob in the land of Canaan.

(Genesis 50:8)

And all the house of Joseph, and his brothers, and his father's house: only their little ones, and their flocks, and their herds, they left in the land of Goshen.

(Genesis 50:9)

And there went up with him both chariots and horsemen: and it was a very great company.

(Jasher 56:35)
And the sons of Jacob carried the bier upon which he lay; according to all that their father commanded them, so did his sons to him.

(Jasher 56:36)
And the bier was of pure gold, and it was inlaid round about with onyx stones and bdellium; and the covering of the bier was gold woven work, joined with threads, and over them were hooks of onyx stones and bdellium.

(Jasher 56:37)
And Joseph placed upon the head of his father Jacob a large golden crown, and he put a golden scepter in his hand, and they surrounded the bier as was the custom of kings during their lives.

(Jasher 56:38)
And all the troops of Egypt went before him in this array, at first all the mighty men of Pharaoh, and the mighty men of Joseph, and after them the rest of the inhabitants of Egypt, and they were all girded with swords and equipped with coats of mail, and the trappings of war were upon them.

(Jasher 56:39)
And all the weepers and mourners went at a distance opposite to the bier, going and weeping and lamenting, and the rest of the people went after the bier.

(Jasher 56:40)
And Joseph and his household went together near the bier barefooted and weeping, and the rest of Joseph's servants went around him; each man had his ornaments upon him, and they were all armed with their weapons of war.

(Jasher 56:41)
And fifty of Jacob's servants went in front of the bier, and they strewed along the road myrrh and aloes, and all manner of perfume, and all the sons of Jacob that carried the bier walked upon the perfumery, and the servants of Jacob went before them strewing the perfume along the road.

(Genesis 50:10) (Jasher 56:42)
And Joseph went up with a heavy camp, and they did after this manner every day until they reached the land of Canaan,

and they came to the threshing floor of Atad, which is beyond Jordan, and there they mourned with a great and very sore lamentation: and he made a mourning for his father seven days.

(Jasher 56:43)
And all the kings of Canaan heard of this thing and they all went forth, each man from his house, thirty-one kings of Canaan, and they all came with their men to mourn and weep over Jacob.

(Jasher 56:44)
And all these kings beheld Jacob's bier, and behold Joseph's crown was upon it, and they also put their crowns upon the bier, and encircled it with crowns.

(Jasher 56:45)
And all these kings made in that place a great and heavy mourning with the sons of Jacob and Egypt over Jacob, for all the kings of Canaan knew the valor of Jacob and his sons.

(Jasher 56:46)
And the report reached Esau, saying, Jacob died in Egypt, and his sons and all Egypt are conveying him to the land of Canaan to bury him.

(Jasher 56:47)
And Esau heard this thing, and he was dwelling in mount Seir, and he rose up with his sons and all his people and all his household, a people exceedingly great, and they came to mourn and weep over Jacob.

(Jasher 56:48)
And it came to pass, when Esau came he mourned for his

brother Jacob, and all Egypt and all Canaan again rose up and mourned a great mourning with Esau over Jacob in that place.

(Genesis 50:11)

And when the inhabitants of the land, the Canaanites, saw the mourning in the floor of Atad, they said, This is a grievous mourning to the Egyptians: why the name of it was called Abelmizraim, which is beyond Jordan.

(Genesis 50:12)

And his sons did to him according as he commanded them:

(Genesis 50:13...) (Jasher 56:49)

For Joseph and his brothers brought their father Jacob from that place and Jacob's sons carried him into the land of Canaan, and they went to Hebron to bury Jacob in the cave by his fathers.

(Jasher 56:50)

And they came to Kireath-arba, to the cave, and as they came Esau stood with his sons against Joseph and his brothers as a hindrance in the cave, saying, Jacob shall not be buried therein, for it belongs to us and to our father.

(Jasher 56:51)

And Joseph and his brothers heard the words of Esau's sons, and they were exceedingly wroth, and Joseph approached to Esau, saying, What is this thing which they have spoken? Surely my father Jacob bought it from you for great riches after the death of Isaac, now twenty-five years ago, and also all the land of Canaan he bought from you and from your sons, and your seed after you.

(Jasher 56:52)
And Jacob bought it for his sons and his seed after him for an inheritance forever, and why do you speak these things this day?

(Jasher 56:53)
And Esau answered, saying, You speak falsely and utter lies, for I sold not anything belonging to me in all this land, as you say, neither did my brother Jacob buy aught belonging to me in this land.

(Jasher 56:54)
And Esau spoke these things in order to deceive Joseph with his words, for Esau knew that Joseph was not present in those days when Esau sold all belonging to him in the land of Canaan to Jacob.

(Jasher 56:55)
And Joseph said to Esau, Surely my father inserted these things with you in the record of purchase, and testified the record with witnesses, and behold it is with us in Egypt.

(Jasher 56:56)
And Esau answered, saying to him, Bring the record, all that you will find in the record, so will we do.

(Jasher 56:57)
And Joseph called to Naphtali his brother, and he said, Hurry quickly, do not stay, and run I pray you to Egypt and bring all the records; the record of the purchase, the sealed record and the open record, and also all the first records in which all the transactions of the birth-right are written, fetch you.

(Jasher 56:58)
And you shall bring them here to us, that we may know from them all the words of Esau and his sons which they spoke this day.

(Jasher 56:59)
And Naphtali hearkened to the voice of Joseph and he hastened and ran to go down to Egypt, and Naphtali was lighter on foot than any of the stags that were upon the wilderness, for he would go upon ears of corn without crushing them.

(Jasher 56:60)
And when Esau saw that Naphtali had gone to fetch the records, he and his sons increased their resistance against the cave, and Esau and all his people rose up against Joseph and his brothers to battle.

(Jasher 56:61)
And all the sons of Jacob and the people of Egypt fought with Esau and his men, and the sons of Esau and his people were smitten before the sons of Jacob, and the sons of Jacob slew of Esau's people forty men.

(Jasher 56:62)
And Chushim the son of Dan, the son of Jacob, was at that time with Jacob's sons, but he was about a hundred cubits distant from the place of battle, for he remained with the children of Jacob's sons by Jacob's bier to guard it.

(Jasher 56:63)
And Chushim was dumb and deaf, still he understood the voice of consternation among men.

(Jasher 56:64)
And he asked, saying, Why do you not bury the dead, and what is this great consternation? And they answered him the words of Esau and his sons; and he ran to Esau in the midst of the battle, and he slew Esau with a sword, and he cut off his head, and it sprang to a distance, and Esau fell among the people of the battle.

(...Genesis 50:13) (Jasher 56:65, 66)
And when Chushim did this thing the sons of Jacob prevailed over the sons of Esau, and the sons of Jacob buried their father Jacob by force in the cave of the field of Machpelah, which Abraham bought from the sons of Heth with the field for a possession of a burying place of Ephron the Hittite, before Mamre, and he was buried in very costly garments, and the sons of Esau beheld it.

(Jubilees 45:15)
And Jacob slept with his fathers, and he was buried in the double cave in the land of Canaan, near Abraham his father in the grave which he dug for himself in the double cave in the land of Hebron.

(Jubilees 45:16)
And he gave all his books and the books of his fathers to Levi his son that he might preserve them and renew them for his children until this day.

(Jasher 56:67)
And no king had such honor paid him as Joseph paid to his father at his death, for he buried him with great honor like to the burial of kings.

(Jasher 56:68)
And Joseph and his brothers made a mourning of seven days for their father.

~ ~ ~

(Jasher 57:1)
And it was after this that the sons of Esau waged war with the sons of Jacob, and the sons of Esau fought with the sons of Jacob in Hebron, and Esau was still lying dead, and not buried.

(Jasher 57:2)
And the battle was heavy between them, and the sons of Esau were smitten before the sons of Jacob, and the sons of Jacob slew of the sons of Esau eighty men, and not one died of the people of the sons of Jacob; and the hand of Joseph prevailed over all the people of the sons of Esau, and he took Zepho, the son of Eliphaz, the son of Esau, and fifty of his men captive, and he bound them with chains of iron, and gave them into the hand of his servants to bring them to Egypt.

(Jasher 57:3)
And it came to pass when the sons of Jacob had taken Zepho and his people captive, all those that remained were greatly afraid of their lives from the house of Esau, lest they should also be taken captive, and they all fled with Eliphaz the son of Esau and his people, with Esau's body, and they went on their road to Mount Seir.

(Jasher 57:4)
And they came to Mount Seir and they buried Esau in Seir,

but they had not brought his head with them to Seir, for it was buried in that place where the battle had been in Hebron.

(Jasher 57:5)
And it came to pass when the sons of Esau had fled from before the sons of Jacob, the sons of Jacob pursued them to the borders of Seir, but they did not slay a single man from among them when they pursued them, for Esau's body which they carried with them excited their confusion, so they fled and the sons of Jacob turned back from them and came up to the place where their brothers were in Hebron, and they remained there on that day, and on the next day until they rested from the battle.

(Genesis 50:14)
And Joseph returned into Egypt, he, and his brothers, and all that went up with him to bury his father, after he had buried his father.

(Genesis 50:15)
And when Joseph's brothers saw that their father was dead, they said, Joseph will peradventure hate us, and will certainly requite us all the evil which we did to him.

(Genesis 50:16)
And they sent a messenger to Joseph, saying, Your father commanded before he died, saying,

(Genesis 50:17)
So shall you say to Joseph, Forgive, I pray now, the trespass of your brothers, and their sin; for they did to you evil: and now, we pray, forgive the trespass of the servants of the God of your father. And Joseph wept when they spoke to him.

(Genesis 50:18)
And his brothers also went and fell down before his face; and they said, Behold, we be your servants.

(Genesis 50:19)
And Joseph said to them, Fear not: for am I in the place of God?

(Genesis 50:20)
But as for you, you thought evil against me; but God meant it to good, to bring to pass, as it is this day, to save much people alive.

(Genesis 50:21)
Now therefore fear you not: I will nourish you, and your little ones. And he comforted them, and spoke kindly to them.

(Jasher 57:6)
And it came to pass on the third day they assembled all the sons of Seir the Horite, and they assembled all the children of the east, a multitude of people like the sand of the sea, and they went and came down to Egypt to fight with Joseph and his brothers, in order to deliver their brothers.

(Jasher 57:7)
And Joseph and all the sons of Jacob heard that the sons of Esau and the children of the east had come upon them to battle in order to deliver their brothers.

(Jasher 57:8)
And Joseph and his brothers and the strong men of Egypt went forth and fought in the city of Rameses, and Joseph and his brothers dealt out a tremendous blow among the sons of

Esau and the children of the east.

(Jasher 57:9)
And they slew of them six hundred thousand men, and they slew among them all the mighty men of the children of Seir the Horite; there were only a few of them left, and they slew also a great many of the children of the east, and of the children of Esau; and Eliphaz the son of Esau, and the children of the east all fled before Joseph and his brothers.

(Jasher 57:10)
And Joseph and his brothers pursued them until they came to Succoth, and they yet slew of them in Succoth thirty men, and the rest escaped and they fled each to his city.

(Jasher 57:11)
And Joseph and his brothers and the mighty men of Egypt turned back from them with joy and cheerfulness of heart, for they had smitten all their enemies.

(Jasher 57:12)
And Zepho the son of Eliphaz and his men were still slaves in Egypt to the sons of Jacob, and their pains increased.

(Jasher 57:13)
And when the sons of Esau and the sons of Seir returned to their land, the sons of Seir saw that they had all fallen into the hands of the sons of Jacob, and the people of Egypt, on account of the battle of the sons of Esau.

(Jasher 57:14)
And the sons of Seir said to the sons of Esau, You have seen and therefore, you know that this camp was on your account, and not one mighty man or an adept in war remains.

(Jasher 57:15)
Now therefore go forth from our land, go from us to the land of Canaan to the land of the dwelling of your fathers; wherefore shall your children inherit the effects of our children in latter days?

(Jasher 57:16)
And the children of Esau would not listen to the children of Seir, and the children of Seir considered to make war with them.

(Jasher 57:17)
And the children of Esau sent secretly to Angeas king of Africa, the same is Dinhabah, saying,

(Jasher 57:18)
Send to us some of your men and let them come to us, and we will fight together with the children of Seir the Horite, for they have resolved to fight with us to drive us away from the land.

(Jasher 57:19)
And Angeas king of Dinhabah did so, for he was in those days friendly to the children of Esau, and Angeas sent five hundred valiant infantry to the children of Esau, and eight hundred cavalry.

(Jasher 57:20)
And the children of Seir sent to the children of the east and to the children of Midian, saying, You have seen what the children of Esau have done to us, upon whose account we are almost all destroyed, in their battle with the sons of Jacob.

(Jasher 57:21)
Now therefore come to us and assist us, and we will fight

them together, and we will drive them from the land and be avenged of the cause of our brothers who died for their sakes in their battle with their brothers the sons of Jacob.

(Jasher 57:22)
And all the children of the east listened to the children of Seir, and they came to them about eight hundred men with drawn swords, and the children of Esau fought with the children of Seir at that time in the wilderness of Paran.

(Jasher 57:23)
And the children of Seir prevailed then over the sons of Esau, and the children of Seir slew on that day of the children of Esau in that battle about two hundred men of the people of Angeas king of Dinhabah.

(Jasher 57:24)
And on the second day the children of Esau came again to fight a second time with the children of Seir, and the battle was sore upon the children of Esau this second time, and it troubled them greatly on account of the children of Seir.

(Jasher 57:25)
And when the children of Esau saw that the children of Seir were more powerful than they were, some men of the children of Esau turned and assisted the children of Seir their enemies.

(Jasher 57:26)
And there fell yet of the people of the children of Esau in the second battle fifty-eight men of the people at Angeas king of Dinhabah.

(Jasher 57:27)
And on the third day the children of Esau heard that some of

their brothers had turned from them to fight against them in the second battle; and the children of Esau mourned when they heard this thing.

(Jasher 57:28)
And they said, What shall we do to our brothers who turned from us to assist the children of Seir our enemies? And the children of Esau again sent to Angeas king of Dinhabah, saying,

(Jasher 57:29)
Send to us again other men that with them we may fight with the children of Seir, for they have already twice been heavier than we were.

(Jasher 57:30)
And Angeas again sent to the children of Esau about six hundred valiant men, and they came to assist the children of Esau.

(Jasher 57:31)
And in ten days' time the children of Esau again waged war with the children of Seir in the wilderness of Paran, and the battle was very severe upon the children of Seir, and the children of Esau prevailed at this time over the children of Seir, and the children of Seir were smitten before the children of Esau, and the children of Esau slew from them about two thousand men.

(Jasher 57:32)
And all the mighty men of the children of Seir died in this battle, and there only remained their young children that were left in their cities.

(Jasher 57:33)
And all Midian and the children of the east betook themselves to flight from the battle, and they left the children of Seir and fled when they saw that the battle was severe upon them, and the children of Esau pursued all the children of the east until they reached their land.

(Jasher 57:34)
And the children of Esau slew yet of them about two hundred and fifty men and from the people of the children of Esau there fell in that battle about thirty men, but this evil came upon them through their brothers turning from them to assist the children of Seir the Horite, and the children of Esau again heard of the evil doings of their brothers, and they again mourned on account of this thing.

(Jasher 57:35)
And it came to pass after the battle, the children of Esau turned back and came home to Seir, and the children of Esau slew those who had remained in the land of the children of Seir; they slew also their wives and little ones, they left not a soul alive except fifty young lads and damsels whom they suffered to live, and the children of Esau did not put them to death, and the lads became their slaves, and the damsels they took for wives.

(Jasher 57:36)
And the children of Esau dwelt in Seir in the place of the children of Seir, and they inherited their land and took possession of it.

(Jasher 57:37)
And the children of Esau took all belonging in the land to the children of Seir, also their flocks, their bullocks and their goods, and all belonging to the children of Seir, the children

of Esau took, and the children of Esau dwelt in Seir in the place of the children of Seir to this day, and the children of Esau divided the land into divisions to the five sons of Esau, according to their families.

(Jasher 57:38)
And it came to pass in those days, that the children of Esau resolved to crown a king over them in the land of which they became possessed. And they said to each other, Not so, for he shall reign over us in our land, and we shall be under his counsel and he shall fight our battles, against our enemies, and they did so.

(Jasher 57:39)
And all the children of Esau swore, saying, That none of their brothers should ever reign over them, but a strange man who is not of their brothers, for the souls of all the children of Esau were embittered every man against his son, brother and friend, on account of the evil they sustained from their brothers when they fought with the children of Seir.

(Jasher 57:40)
Therefore, the sons of Esau swore, saying, From that day forward they would not choose a king from their brothers, but one from a strange land to this day.

(Jasher 57:41)
And there was a man there from the people of Angeas king of Dinhabah; his name was Bela the son of Beor, who was a very valiant man, beautiful and comely and wise in all wisdom, and a man of sense and counsel; and there was none of the people of Angeas like to him.

(Jasher 57:42)
And all the children of Esau took him and anointed him and they crowned him for a king, and they bowed down to him, and they said to him, May the king live, may the king live.

(Jasher 57:43)
And they spread out the sheet, and they brought him each man earrings of gold and silver or rings or bracelets, and they made him very rich in silver and in gold, in onyx stones and bdellium, and they made him a royal throne, and they placed a regal crown upon his head, and they built a palace for him and he dwelt therein, and he became king over all the children of Esau.

(Jasher 57:44)
And the people of Angeas took their hire for their battle from the children of Esau, and they went and returned at that time to their master in Dinhabah.

(Jasher 57:45)
And Bela reigned over the children of Esau thirty years, and the children of Esau dwelt in the land instead of the children of Seir, and they dwelt securely in their stead to this day.

~ ~ ~

(Jasher 58:1)
And it came to pass in the thirty-second year of the Israelites going down to Egypt, that is in the seventy-first year of the life of Joseph, in that year died Pharaoh king of Egypt, and Magron his son reigned in his stead.

(Jasher 58:2)
And Pharaoh commanded Joseph before his death to be a father to his son, Magron, and that Magron should be under the care of Joseph and under his counsel.

(Jasher 58:3)
And all Egypt consented to this thing that Joseph should be king over them, for all the Egyptians loved Joseph as of heretofore, only Magron the son of Pharaoh sat upon, his father's throne, and he became king in those days in his father's stead.

(Jasher 58:4)
Magron was forty-one years old when he began to reign, and forty years he reigned in Egypt, and all Egypt called his name Pharaoh after the name of his father, as it was their custom to do in Egypt to every king that reigned over them.

(Jasher 58:5)
And it came to pass when Pharaoh reigned in his father's stead, he placed the laws of Egypt and all the affairs of government in the hand of Joseph, as his father had commanded him.

(Jasher 58:6)
And Joseph became king over Egypt, for he superintended over all Egypt, and all Egypt was under his care and under his counsel, for all Egypt inclined to Joseph after the death of Pharaoh, and they loved him exceedingly to reign over them.

(Jasher 58:7)
But there were some people among them, who did not like him, saying, No stranger shall reign over us; still the whole government of Egypt devolved in those days upon Joseph, after the death of Pharaoh, he being the regulator, doing as he

liked throughout the land without any one interfering.

(Jasher 58:8)
And all Egypt was under the care of Joseph, and Joseph made war with all his surrounding enemies, and he subdued them; also, all the land and all the Philistines, to the borders of Canaan, Joseph subdued, and they were all under his power and they gave a yearly tax to Joseph.

(Jasher 58:9)
And Pharaoh king of Egypt sat upon his throne in his father's stead, but he was under the control and counsel of Joseph, as he was at first under the control of his father.

(Jasher 58:10)
Neither did he reign but in the land of Egypt only, under the counsel of Joseph, but Joseph reigned over the whole country at that time, from Egypt to the great river Perath.

(Jasher 58:11)
And Joseph was successful in all his ways, and the Lord was with him, and the Lord gave Joseph additional wisdom, and honor, and glory, and love toward him in the hearts of the Egyptians and throughout the land, and Joseph reigned over the whole country forty years.

(Jasher 58:12)
And all the countries of the Philistines and Canaan and Zidon, and on the other side of Jordan, brought presents to Joseph all his days, and the whole country was in the hand of Joseph, and they brought to him a yearly tribute as it was regulated, for Joseph had fought against all his surrounding enemies and subdued them, and the whole country was in the hand of Joseph, and Joseph sat securely upon his throne in Egypt.

(Jasher 58:13)
And also, all his brothers the sons of Jacob dwelt securely in the land, all the days of Joseph, and they were fruitful and multiplied exceedingly in the land, and they served the Lord all their days, as their father Jacob had commanded them.

(Jasher 58:14)
And it came to pass at the end of many days and years, when the children of Esau were dwelling quietly in their land with Bela their king, that the children of Esau were fruitful and multiplied in the land, and they resolved to go and fight with the sons of Jacob and all Egypt, and to deliver their brother Zepho, the son of Eliphaz, and his men, for they were yet in those days slaves to Joseph.

(Jasher 58:15)
And the children of Esau sent to all the children of the east, and they made peace with them, and all the children of the east came to them to go with the children of Esau to Egypt to battle.

(Jasher 58:16)
And there came also to them of the people of Angeas, king of Dinhabah, and they also sent to the children of Ishmael and they also came to them.

(Jasher 58:17)
And all this people assembled and came to Seir to assist the children of Esau in their battle, and this camp was very large and heavy with people, numerous as the sand of the sea, about eight hundred thousand men, infantry and cavalry, and all these troops went down to Egypt to fight with the sons of Jacob, and they encamped by Rameses.

(Jasher 58:18)
And Joseph went forth with his brothers with the mighty men of Egypt, about six hundred men, and they fought with them in the land of Rameses; and the sons of Jacob at that time again fought with the children of Esau, in the fiftieth year of the sons of Jacob going down to Egypt, that is the thirtieth year of the reign of Bela over the children of Esau in Seir.

(Jasher 58:19)
And the Lord gave all the mighty men of Esau and the children of the east into the hand of Joseph and his brothers, and the people of the children of Esau and the children of the east were smitten before Joseph.

(Jasher 58:20)
And of the people of Esau and the children of the east that were slain, there fell before the sons of Jacob about two hundred thousand men, and their king Bela the son of Beor fell with them in the battle, and when the children of Esau saw that their king had fallen in battle and was dead, their hands became weak in the combat.

(Jasher 58:21)
And Joseph and his brothers and all Egypt were still smiting the people of the house of Esau, and all Esau's people were afraid of the sons of Jacob and fled from before them.

(Jasher 58:22)
And Joseph and his brothers and all Egypt pursued them a day's journey, and they slew yet from them about three hundred men, continuing to smite them in the road; and they afterward turned back from them.

(Jasher 58:23)
And Joseph and all his brothers returned to Egypt, not one man was missing from them, but of the Egyptians there fell twelve men.

(Jasher 58:24)
And when Joseph returned to Egypt he ordered Zepho and his men to be additionally bound, and they bound them in irons and they increased their grief.

(Jasher 58:25)
And all the people of the children of Esau, and the children of the east, returned in shame each to his city, for all the mighty men that were with them had fallen in battle.

(Jasher 58:26)
And when the children of Esau saw that their king had died in battle they hastened and took a man from the people of the children of the east; his name was Jobab the son of Zarach, from the land of Botzrah, and they caused him to reign over them instead of Bela their king.

(Jasher 58:27)
And Jobab sat upon the throne of Bela as king in his stead, and Jobab reigned in Edom over all the children of Esau ten years, and the children of Esau went no more to fight with the sons of Jacob from that day forward, for the sons of Esau knew the valor of the sons of Jacob, and they were greatly afraid of them.

(Jasher 58:28)
But from that day forward the children of Esau hated the sons of Jacob, and the hatred and enmity were very strong between them all the days, to this day.

(Jasher 58:29)
And it came to pass after this, at the end of ten years, Jobab, the son of Zarach, from Botzrah, died, and the children of Esau took a man whose name was Chusham, from the land of Teman, and they made him king over them instead of Jobab, and Chusham reigned in Edom over all the children of Esau for twenty years.

(Jasher 58:30)
And Joseph, king of Egypt, and his brothers, and all the children of Israel dwelt securely in Egypt in those days, together with all the children of Joseph and his brothers, having no hindrance or evil accident and the land of Egypt was at that time at rest from war in the days of Joseph and his brothers.

(Genesis 50:22...) (...Jasher 59:19) (Jubilees 46:1)
And it came to pass that after Jacob died the children of Israel multiplied in the land of Egypt. And Joseph dwelt securely in Egypt, he, and his father's house: and they ate of the best of Egypt and they became a great nation, and they were of one accord in heart, so that brother loved brother and every man helped his brother, and they increased abundantly and multiplied exceedingly, ten weeks of years, all the days of the life of Joseph.

(Jubilees 46:2)
And there was no Satan nor any evil all the days of the life of Joseph which he lived after his father Jacob, for all the Egyptians honored the children of Israel all the days of the life of Joseph.

(Jasher 59:20) (Jubilees 46:3...)
And Joseph lived in the land of Canaan seventeen years, and ten years he was a servant, and three years in prison.

So Joseph lived in the land of Egypt ninety-three years, and Joseph was reigning under the king over all the land of Egypt eighty years.

(...Genesis 50:22) (...Jubilees 46:3)

And Joseph lived a hundred and ten years.

(Genesis 50:23)

And Joseph saw Ephraim's children of the third generation: the children also of Machir the son of Manasseh were brought up on Joseph's knees.

(Jasher 59:21)

And when the days of Joseph drew near that he should die, he sent and called for his brothers and all his father's household, and they all came together and sat before him.

(Genesis 50:24) (Jasher 59:22)

And Joseph said to his brothers, and to the whole of his father's household, Behold I die: and God will surely visit you, and bring you out of this land to the land which he swore your fathers, to Abraham, to Isaac, and to Jacob, to give to them.

(Jasher 59:23)

And it shall be when God shall visit you to bring you up from here to the land of your fathers, then bring up my bones with you from here.

(Genesis 50:25) (Jasher 59:24) (Jubilees 46:5)

And Joseph commanded the children of Israel before he died and took an oath of the children of Israel for their seed after them, saying, God will surely visit you, and you shall carry up my bones from hence.

(Jubilees 46:6)
And he made them swear regarding his bones, for he knew that the Egyptians would not again bring forth and bury him in the land of Canaan, for Makamaron, king of Canaan, while dwelling in the land of Assyria, fought in the valley with the king of Egypt and slew him there, and pursued after the Egyptians to the gates of ʻErmon.

(Jubilees 46:7)
But he was not able to enter, for another, a new king, had become king of Egypt, and he was stronger than he, and he returned to the land of Canaan, and the gates of Egypt were closed, and none went out and none came into Egypt.

(Genesis 50:26...) (Jasher 59:25, 26) (Jubilees 46:8...)
And it came to pass after this that Joseph died in that year, in the forty-sixth jubilee, in the sixth week, in the second year, the seventy-first year of the Israelites going down to Egypt. And Joseph was a hundred and ten years old when he died in the land of Egypt, and all his brothers and all his servants rose up and they embalmed him, as was their custom, and his brothers and all Egypt mourned over him for seventy days.

(...Genesis 50:26) (Jasher 59:27) (...Jubilees 46:8)
And they put Joseph in a coffin filled with spices and all sorts of perfume, and they buried him in the land of Egypt by the side of the river, that is Sihor, and his sons and all his brothers, and the whole of his father's household made a seven day's mourning for him.

(Jubilees 46:4, ...8)
And Joseph died and all his brothers died after him and all that generation.

(Jasher 59:28)
And it came to pass after the death of Joseph, all the Egyptians began in those days to rule over the children of Israel, and Pharaoh, king of Egypt, who reigned in his father's stead, took all the laws of Egypt and conducted the whole government of Egypt under his counsel, and he reigned securely over his people.

Epilogue

(Jasher 60:1)
And when the year came round, being the seventy-second year from the Israelites going down to Egypt, after the death of Joseph, Zepho, the son of Eliphaz, the son of Esau, fled from Egypt, he and his men, and they went away.

(Jasher 60:2)
And he came to Africa, which is Dinhabah, to Angeas king of Africa, and Angeas received them with great honor, and he made Zepho the captain of his host.

(Jasher 60:3)
And Zepho found favor in the sight of Angeas and in the sight of his people, and Zepho was captain of the host to Angeas king of Africa for many days.

(Jasher 60:4)
And Zepho enticed Angeas king of Africa to collect all his army to go and fight with the Egyptians, and with the sons of Jacob, and to avenge of them the cause of his brothers.

(Jasher 60:5)
But Angeas would not listen to Zepho to do this thing, for Angeas knew the strength of the sons of Jacob, and what they had done to his army in their warfare with the children of Esau.

(Jasher 60:6)
And Zepho was in those days very great in the sight of Angeas

and in the sight of all his people, and he continually enticed them to make war against Egypt, but they would not.

(Jasher 60:7)
And it came to pass in those days there was in the land of Chittim a man in the city of Puzimna, whose name was Uzu, and he became degenerately deified by the children of Chittim, and the man died and had no son, only one daughter whose name was Jania.

(Jasher 60:8)
And the damsel was exceedingly beautiful, comely and intelligent, there was none seen like to her for beauty and wisdom throughout the land.

(Jasher 60:9)
And the people of Angeas king of Africa saw her and they came and praised her to him, and Angeas sent to the children of Chittim, and he requested to take her to himself for a wife, and the people of Chittim consented to give her to him for a wife.

(Jasher 60:10)
And when the messengers of Angeas were going forth from the land of Chittim to take their journey, behold the messengers of Turnus king of Bibentu came to Chittim, for Turnus king of Bibentu also sent his messengers to request Jania for him, to take to himself for a wife, for all his men had also praised her to him, therefore he sent all his servants to her.

(Jasher 60:11)
And the servants of Turnus came to Chittim, and they asked for Jania, to be taken to Turnus their king for a wife.

(Jasher 60:12)
And the people of Chittim said to them, We cannot give her, because Angeas king of Africa desired her to take her to him for a wife before you came, and that we should give her to him, and now therefore we cannot do this thing to deprive Angeas of the damsel in order to give her to Turnus.

(Jasher 60:13)
For we are greatly afraid of Angeas lest he come in battle against us and destroy us, and Turnus your master will not be able to deliver us from his hand.

(Jasher 60:14)
And when the messengers of Turnus heard all the words of the children of Chittim, they turned back to their master and told him all the words of the children of Chittim.

(Jasher 60:15)
And the children of Chittim sent a memorial to Angeas, saying, Behold Turnus has sent for Jania to take her to him for a wife, and thus have we answered him; and we heard that he has collected his whole army to go to war against you, and he intends to pass by the road of Sardunia to fight against your brother Lucus, and after that he will come to fight against you.

(Jasher 60:16)
And Angeas heard the words of the children of Chittim which they sent to him in the record, and his anger was kindled and he rose up and assembled his whole army and came through the islands of the sea, the road to Sardunia, to his brother Lucus king of Sardunia.

(Jasher 60:17)
And Niblos, the son of Lucus, heard that his uncle Angeas was

coming, and he went out to meet him with a heavy army, and he kissed him and embraced him, and Niblos said to Angeas, When you ask my father after his welfare, when I shall go with you to fight with Turnus, ask of him to make me captain of his host, and Angeas did so, and he came to his brother and his brother came to meet him, and he asked him after his welfare.

(Jasher 60:18)
And Angeas asked his brother Lucus after his welfare, and to make his son Niblos captain of his host, and Lucus did so, and Angeas and his brother Lucus rose up and they went toward Turnus to battle, and there was with them a great army and a heavy people.

(Jasher 60:19)
And he came in ships, and they came into the province of Ashtorash, and behold Turnus came toward them, for he went forth to Sardunia, and intended to destroy it and afterward to pass on from there to Angeas to fight with him.

(Jasher 60:20)
And Angeas and Lucus his brother met Turnus in the valley of Canopia, and the battle was strong and mighty between them in that place.

(Jasher 60:21)
And the battle was severe upon Lucus king of Sardunia, and all his army fell, and Niblos his son fell also in that battle.

(Jasher 60:22)
And his uncle Angeas commanded his servants and they made a golden coffin for Niblos and they put him into it, and Angeas again waged battle toward Turnus, and Angeas was stronger than he, and he slew him, and he smote all his people with the

edge of the sword, and Angeas avenged the cause of Niblos his brother's son and the cause of the army of his brother Lucus.

(Jasher 60:23)
And when Turnus died, the hands of those that survived the battle became weak, and they fled from before Angeas and Lucus his brother.

(Jasher 60:24)
And Angeas and his brother Lucus pursued them to the highroad, which is between Alphanu and Romah, and they slew the whole army of Turnus with the edge of the sword.

(Jasher 60:25)
And Lucus king of Sardunia commanded his servants that they should make a coffin of brass, and that they should place therein the body of his son Niblos, and they buried him in that place.

(Jasher 60:26)
And they built upon it a high tower there upon the highroad, and they called its name after the name of Niblos to this day, and they also buried Turnus king of Bibentu there in that place with Niblos.

(Jasher 60:27)
And behold upon the highroad between Alphanu and Romah the grave of Niblos is on one side and the grave of Turnus on the other, and a pavement between them to this day.

(Jasher 60:28)
And when Niblos was buried, Lucus his father returned with his army to his land Sardunia, and Angeas his brother king of

Africa went with his people to the city of Bibentu, that is the city of Turnus.

(Jasher 60:29)
And the inhabitants of Bibentu heard of his fame and they were greatly afraid of him, and they went forth to meet him with weeping and supplication, and the inhabitants of Bibentu entreated of Angeas not to slay them nor destroy their city; and he did so, for Bibentu was in those days reckoned as one of the cities of the children of Chittim; therefore, he did not destroy the city.

(Jasher 60:30)
But from that day forward the troops of the king of Africa would go to Chittim to spoil and plunder it, and whenever they went, Zepho the captain of the host of Angeas would go with them.

(Jasher 60:31)
And it was after this that Angeas turned with his army and they came to the city of Puzimna, and Angeas took thence Jania the daughter of Uzu for a wife and brought her to his city to Africa.

~ ~ ~ ~ ~

(Jasher 61:1)
And it came to pass at that time Pharaoh king of Egypt commanded all his people to make for him a strong palace in Egypt.

(Jasher 61:2)
And he also commanded the sons of Jacob to assist the Egyptians in the building, and the Egyptians made a beautiful

and elegant palace for a royal habitation, and he dwelt therein and he renewed his government and he reigned securely.

(Jasher 61:3)
And Zebulun the son of Jacob died in that year, that is the seventy-second year of the going down of the Israelites to Egypt, and Zebulun died a hundred and fourteen years old, and was put into a coffin and given into the hands of his children.

(Jasher 61:4)
And in the seventy-fifth year died his brother Simeon, he was a hundred and twenty years old at his death, and he was also put into a coffin and given into the hands of his children.

(Jasher 61:5)
And Zepho the son of Eliphaz the son of Esau, captain of the host to Angeas king of Dinhabah, was still daily enticing Angeas to prepare for battle to fight with the sons of Jacob in Egypt, and Angeas was unwilling to do this thing, for his servants had related to him all the might of the sons of Jacob, what they had done to them in their battle with the children of Esau.

(Jasher 61:6)
And Zepho was in those days daily enticing Angeas to fight with the sons of Jacob in those days.

(Jasher 61:7)
And after some time Angeas hearkened to the words of Zepho and consented to him to fight with the sons of Jacob in Egypt, and Angeas got all his people in order, a people numerous as the sand which is upon the sea shore, and he formed his resolution to go to Egypt to battle.

(Jasher 61:8)
And among the servants of Angeas was a youth of fifteen years old, Balaam the son of Beor was his name and the youth was very wise and understood the art of witchcraft.

(Jasher 61:9)
And Angeas said to Balaam, Conjure for us, I pray you, with the witchcraft, that we may know who will prevail in this battle to which we are now proceeding.

(Jasher 61:10)
And Balaam ordered that they should bring him wax, and he made thereof the likeness of chariots and horsemen representing the army of Angeas and the army of Egypt, and he put them in the cunningly prepared waters that he had for that purpose, and he took in his hand the boughs of myrtle trees, and he exercised his cunning, and he joined them over the water, and there appeared to him in the water the resembling images of the hosts of Angeas falling before the resembling images of the Egyptians and the sons of Jacob.

(Jasher 61:11)
And Balaam told this thing to Angeas, and Angeas despaired and did not arm himself to go down to Egypt to battle, and he remained in his city.

(Jasher 61:12)
And when Zepho the son of Eliphaz saw that Angeas despaired of going forth to battle with the Egyptians, Zepho fled from Angeas from Africa, and he went and came to Chittim.

(Jasher 61:13)
And all the people of Chittim received him with great honor, and they hired him to fight their battles all the days, and Zepho

became exceedingly rich in those days, and the troops of the king of Africa still spread themselves in those days, and the children of Chittim assembled and went to Mount Cuptizia on account of the troops of Angeas king of Africa, who were advancing upon them.

(Jasher 61:14)
And it was one day that Zepho lost a young heifer, and he went to seek it, and he heard it lowing round about the mountain.

(Jasher 61:15)
And Zepho went and he saw and behold there was a large cave at the bottom of the mountain, and there was a great stone there at the entrance of the cave, and Zepho split the stone and he came into the cave and he looked and behold, a large animal was devouring the ox; from the middle upward it resembled a man, and from the middle downward it resembled an animal, and Zepho rose up against the animal and slew it with his swords.

(Jasher 61:16)
And the inhabitants of Chittim heard of this thing, and they rejoiced exceedingly, and they said, What shall we do to this man who has slain this animal that devoured our cattle?

(Jasher 61:17)
And they all assembled to consecrate one day in the year to him, and they called the name thereof Zepho after his name, and they brought to him drink offerings year after year on that day, and they brought to him gifts.

(Jasher 61:18)
At that time Jania the daughter of Uzu wife of king Angeas became ill, and her illness was heavily felt by Angeas and his

officers, and Angeas said to his wise men, What shall I do to Jania and how shall I heal her from her illness? And his wise men said to him, Because the air of our country is not like the air of the land of Chittim, and our water is not like their water, therefore from this has the queen become ill.

(Jasher 61:19)
For through the change of air and water she became ill, and also because in her country she drank only the water which came from Purmah, which her ancestors had brought up with bridges.

(Jasher 61:20)
And Angeas commanded his servants, and they brought to him in vessels of the waters of Purmah belonging to Chittim, and they weighed those waters with all the waters of the land of Africa, and they found those waters lighter than the waters of Africa.

(Jasher 61:21)
And Angeas saw this thing, and he commanded all his officers to assemble the hewers of stone in thousands and tens of thousands, and they hewed stone without number, and the builders came and they built an exceedingly strong bridge, and they conveyed the spring of water from the land of Chittim to Africa, and those waters were for Jania the queen and for all her concerns, to drink from and to bake, wash and bathe therewith, and also to water therewith all seed from which food can be obtained, and all fruit of the ground.

(Jasher 61:22)
And the king commanded that they should bring of the soil of Chittim in large ships, and they also brought stones to build therewith, and the builders built palaces for Jania the queen, and the queen became healed of her illness.

(Jasher 61:23)
And at the revolution of the year the troops of Africa continued coming to the land of Chittim to plunder as usual, and Zepho son of Eliphaz heard their report, and he gave orders concerning them and he fought with them, and they fled before him, and he delivered the land of Chittim from them.

(Jasher 61:24)
And the children of Chittim saw the valor of Zepho, and the children of Chittim resolved and they made Zepho king over them, and he became king over them, and while he reigned they went to subdue the children of Tubal, and all the surrounding islands.

(Jasher 61:25)
And their king Zepho went at their head and they made war with Tubal and the islands, and they subdued them, and when they returned from the battle they renewed his government for him, and they built for him a very large palace for his royal habitation and seat, and they made a large throne for him, and Zepho reigned over the whole land of Chittim and over the land of Italia fifty years.

~ ~ ~ ~ ~

(Jasher 62:1)
In that year, being the seventy-ninth year of the Israelites going down to Egypt, died Reuben the son of Jacob, in the land of Egypt; Reuben was a hundred and twenty-five years old when he died, and they put him into a coffin, and he was given into the hands of his children.

(Jasher 62:2)
And in the eightieth year died his brother Dan; he was a

hundred and twenty years at his death, and he was also put into a coffin and given into the hands of his children.

(Jasher 62:3)
And in that year died Chusham king of Edom, and after him reigned Hadad the son of Bedad, for thirty-five years; and in the eighty-first year died Issachar the son of Jacob, in Egypt, and Issachar was a hundred and twenty-two years old at his death, and he was put into a coffin in Egypt, and given into the hands of his children.

(Jasher 62:4)
And in the eighty-second year died Asher his brother, he was a hundred and twenty- three years old at his death, and he was placed in a coffin in Egypt, and given into the hands of his children.

(Jasher 62:5)
And in the eighty-third year died Gad, he was a hundred and twenty-five years old at his death, and he was put into a coffin in Egypt, and given into the hands of his children.

(Jasher 62:6)
And it came to pass in the eighty-fourth year, that is the fiftieth year of the reign of Hadad, son of Bedad, king of Edom, that Hadad assembled all the children of Esau, and he got his whole army in readiness, about four hundred thousand men, and he directed his way to the land of Moab, and he went to fight with Moab and to make them tributary to him.

(Jasher 62:7)
And the children of Moab heard this thing, and they were very much afraid, and they sent to the children of Midian to assist

them in fighting with Hadad, son of Bedad, king of Edom.

(Jasher 62:8)
And Hadad came to the land of Moab, and Moab and the children of Midian went out to meet him, and they placed themselves in battle array against him in the field of Moab.

(Jasher 62:9)
And Hadad fought with Moab, and there fell of the children of Moab and the children of Midian many slain ones, about two hundred thousand men.

(Jasher 62:10)
And the battle was very severe upon Moab, and when the children of Moab saw that the battle was sore upon them, they weakened their hands and turned their backs, and left the children of Midian to carry on the battle.

(Jasher 62:11)
And the children of Midian knew not the intentions of Moab, but they strengthened themselves in battle and fought with Hadad and all his host, and all Midian fell before him.

(Jasher 62:12)
And Hadad smote all Midian with a heavy smiting, and he slew them with the edge of the sword, he left none remaining of those who came to assist Moab.

(Jasher 62:13)
And when all the children of Midian had perished in battle, and the children at Moab had escaped, Hadad made all Moab at that time tributary to him, and they became under his hand, and they gave a yearly tax as it was ordered, and Hadad turned and went back to his land.

(Jasher 62:14)
And at the revolution of the year, when the rest of the people of Midian that were in the land heard that all their brothers had fallen in battle with Hadad for the sake of Moab, because the children of Moab had turned their backs in battle and left Midian to fight, then five of the princes of Midian resolved with the rest of their brothers who remained in their land, to fight with Moab to avenge the cause of their brothers.

(Jasher 62:15)
And the children of Midian sent to all their brothers the children of the east, and all their brothers, all the children of Keturah came to assist Midian to fight with Moab.

(Jasher 62:16)
And the children of Moab heard this thing, and they were greatly afraid that all the children of the east had assembled together against them for battle, and they the children of Moab sent a memorial to the land of Edom to Hadad the son of Bedad, saying,

(Jasher 62:17)
Come now to us and assist us and we will smite Midian, for they all assembled together and have come against us with all their brothers the children of the east to battle, to avenge the cause of Midian that fell in battle.

(Jasher 62:18)
And Hadad, son of Bedad, king of Edom, went forth with his whole army and went to the land of Moab to fight with Midian, and Midian and the children of the east fought with Moab in the field of Moab, and the battle was very fierce between them.

(Jasher 62:19)
And Hadad smote all the children of Midian and the children of the east with the edge of the sword, and Hadad at that time delivered Moab from the hand of Midian, and those that remained of Midian and of the children of the east fled before Hadad and his army, and Hadad pursued them to their land, and smote them with a very heavy slaughter, and the slain fell in the road.

(Jasher 62:20)
And Hadad delivered Moab from the hand of Midian, for all the children of Midian had fallen by the edge of the sword, and Hadad turned and went back to his land.

(Jasher 62:21)
And from that day forth, the children of Midian hated the children of Moab, because they had fallen in battle for their sake, and there was a great and mighty enmity between them all the days.

(Jasher 62:22)
And all that were found of Midian in the road of the land of Moab perished by the sword of Moab, and all that were found of Moab in the road of the land of Midian, perished by the sword of Midian; thus did Midian to Moab and Moab to Midian for many days.

(Jasher 62:23)
And it came to pass at that time that Judah the son of Jacob died in Egypt, in the eighty- sixth year of Jacob's going down to Egypt, and Judah was a hundred and twenty-nine years old at his death, and they embalmed him and put him into a coffin, and he was given into the hands of his children.

(Jasher 62:24)
And in the eighty-ninth year died Naphtali, he was a hundred and thirty-two years old, and he was put into a coffin and given into the hands of his children.

(Jasher 62:25)
And it came to pass in the ninety-first year of the Israelites going down to Egypt, that is in the thirtieth year of the reign of Zepho the son of Eliphaz, the son of Esau, over the children of Chittim, the children of Africa came upon the children of Chittim to plunder them as usual, but they had not come upon them for these thirteen years.

(Jasher 62:26)
And they came to them in that year, and Zepho the son of Eliphaz went out to them with some of his men and smote them desperately, and the troops of Africa fled from before Zepho and the slain fell before him, and Zepho and his men pursued them, going on and smiting them until they were near to Africa.

(Jasher 62:27)
And Angeas king of Africa heard the thing which Zepho had done, and it vexed him exceedingly, and Angeas was afraid of Zepho all the days.

Final Notes

We hope your journey is enriched and you are blessed through the production of the **Ancient Texts and the Bible** series!

Minister 2 Others would like to hear from you. If you have comments or questions concerning our materials, or if you find errors in our projects, misspellings, or formatting issues. We work hard to provide quality materials, however, sometimes things can squeak by unnoticed. Your feedback is truly appreciated.

We love producing helpful, innovative books and we are grateful for your support! If you have enjoyed this production, please consider writing a review and letting others know about our materials.

If you would like to be updated when we release new books and other materials, please sign up for our e-newsletter on our website.

Thanks!

Minister 2 Others

Minister2others.com

www.ingramcontent.com/pod-product-compliance
Lightning Source LLC
Chambersburg PA
CBHW071803190726
48292CB00008B/2700

* 9 7 8 1 9 4 7 7 5 1 2 3 1 *